Promoting U.S. Economic Relations with Africa

*Report of an Independent Task Force
Sponsored by the
Council on Foreign Relations*

Peggy Dulany and Frank Savage,
Co-Chairs
Salih Booker, Project Director

The Council on Foreign Relations, Inc., a nonprofit, nonpartisan national membership organization founded in 1921, is dedicated to promoting understanding of international affairs through the free and civil exchange of ideas. The Council's members are dedicated to the belief that America's peace and prosperity are firmly linked to that of the world. From this flows the mission of the Council: to foster America's understanding of its fellow members of the international community, near and far, their peoples, cultures, histories, hopes, quarrels, and ambitions, and thus to serve, protect, and advance America's own global interests through study and debate, private and public.

THE COUNCIL TAKES NO INSTITUTIONAL POSITION ON POL-ICY ISSUES AND HAS NO AFFILIATION WITH THE U.S. GOV-ERNMENT. ALL STATEMENTS OF FACT AND EXPRESSIONS OF OPINION CONTAINED IN ALL ITS PUBLICATIONS ARE THE SOLE RESPONSIBILITY OF THE AUTHOR OR AUTHORS.

The Council on Foreign Relations sponsors independent Task Forces from time to time when it believes that a current foreign policy or international economic debate of critical importance to the United States can benefit from the advice of a small group of people of divergent backgrounds and views. Most, but not all, Task Force members are also members of the Council, and the Council provides the group with staff support.

The goal of the Task Force is to reach a consensus on the issue; if a strong and meaningful consensus cannot be reached, the goal is to state concisely alternative positions.

The Statement of the Task Force reflects the general policy thrust and judgments reached by the group, although not all members necessarily subscribe fully to every finding and recommendation.

For further information about the Council or this Task Force, please contact the Public Affairs Office, Council on Foreign Relations, 58 East 68th Street, New York, NY 10021.

CONTENTS

PREFACE AND ACKNOWLEDGMENTS

Rarely in the history of U.S.-Africa relations have America's economic interests in the countries of the African continent received as much high-level attention from policymakers, business people, analysts and the media as they have in 1997. The Independent Task Force on U.S. Economic Relations with Africa, sponsored by the Council on Foreign Relations, played a key role in this process of increasing interest and broadening public education on Africa's growing importance to the United States.

The Independent Task Force on U.S. Economic Relations with Africa was co-chaired by Peggy Dulany and Frank Savage. The Task Force began as a Study Group aimed at exploring the contours of current U.S. economic policy toward Africa. The Study Group was organized to have each of four sessions devoted to one of the key areas of U.S. development cooperation with African countries: economic policy reform, development assistance, trade and investment, and debt. The group was transformed into a Task Force to enable its members to adopt a consensus position and advocate in support of specific new directions for U.S. policy on most of these issues.

The Task Force met twice in New York and twice in Washington. A single meeting was also held in Atlanta with interested Council members and other citizens. In the course of its deliberations, the Task Force consulted with officials of the executive branch, members of Congress and their staff, and other knowledgeable individuals. The following Statement provides the findings and the recommendations of the Task Force. A number of other Council members were also offered the opportunity to sign the Statement.

As Project Director, I wish to thank all the participants for the time and intellectual energy they gave to this endeavor. I especially wish to thank our co-chairs for their commitment to this process and for the leadership they provided the entire group. I also want to thank those who served as speakers at our sessions, Adebayo Adedeji, Kevin Cleaver, Howard Stein, Carol Peasley, Julius Ihonvbere, Ernest Wilson III, Judith Aidoo, and Charles "Mike" Williams. Without the generous support of the Ford Foundation this project would not have been possible. The Atlanta meeting was organized by Senior Fellow Jennifer Seymour Whitaker and Colin Wheeler of the Council's National Program, and hosted at the Carter Center by Ambassador Harry Barnes. Michael Holtzman handled press relations for the Task Force from the Council's New York office. Finally, I particularly want to thank Marilyn Gayton, Research Associate for the Africa Studies Program at the Council, for facilitating all the communications involved in these proceedings and for the fine work she performed as rapporteur and editor of the Task Force Report.

I have included as Background Materials selected readings used to inform our Task Force deliberations. These texts provide helpful analyses of the key components of U.S. economic relations with Africa upon which the Task Force focused its recommendations.

Salih Booker
Project Director

Promoting U.S. Economic Relations with Africa

STATEMENT OF THE TASK FORCE

INTRODUCTION AND SUMMARY

Significant positive developments in Africa have recently created a sense of economic and political renewal throughout much of the continent. Over two-thirds of African countries are implementing economic policy reforms that emphasize growth, private-sector development, and greater openness to the global economy. Aggregate growth rates for these 35 African countries in 1995 and 1996 averaged 5 percent, more than twice the rates of the previous decade. A new generation of leadership in Africa is promoting a reform agenda that offers important opportunities for rapid economic growth and increasing African countries' participation in the global economy. Now that an increasing number of African countries are becoming strong candidates as potential trade and investment partners, the United States should be at the forefront of the industrialized world in pursuit of these new opportunities.

Recognizing the favorable economic and political trends occurring in most African countries, the Council on Foreign Relations—while taking no position on the subject as an organization—sponsored an independent Task Force of distinguished private citizens, committed to strengthening American ties with Africa, to make recommendations on how best to advance mutual U.S. and African interests in the sphere of economic relations.

Despite the renewal in Africa and the quiet expansion of U.S. economic interests on the continent, the prevailing perceptions of Africa's potential remain overwhelmingly negative within parts of the policymaking and business communities, and among the larg-

---

The Statement of the Task Force reflects the general policy thrust and judgments reached by the group, although not all members necessarily subscribe fully to every finding and recommendation.

er American body politic. In the minds of many Americans, economic and political crises in a handful of traumatized countries have tended to obfuscate the impressive growth and political turnarounds occurring in many other African countries. Consequently, the Task Force believes that new opportunities to increase economic ties with Africa will require considerable executive branch leadership if they are to receive the attention and support they deserve.

Prior to this year, American economic interests in Africa have consistently received less attention from U.S. policymakers than those in every other world region. The late Commerce Secretary Ronald Brown's trade missions to the continent, his appointment of a minister counselor for southern Africa, and Vice President Al Gore's efforts in the U.S.- South Africa Bi-National Commission are the main innovations in U.S. economic policy toward Africa in recent years. Outside of these deeds, however, the countries of Africa have been largely excluded from the most dynamic component of the administration's foreign policy, namely, the promotion of U.S. trade and investment in an expanding and increasingly integrated global economy. This is despite the fact that the United States exports more to Africa than to all the newly independent states (NIS) of the former Soviet Union and Eastern Europe combined. In fact, U.S. exports to South Africa alone nearly equaled U.S. sales to Russia and are greater than U.S. exports to all of Eastern Europe.

In light of this history, the Task Force notes with approval the recently increased attention given to African trade and investment issues by both Congress and the administration. However, the Task Force believes that legislative and executive initiatives fall short of offering a new economic policy for Africa that is as comprehensive as is warranted. The Task Force concludes that the United States needs a new economic policy for Africa that integrates *trade and investment*, *aid*, and *debt reduction* in a more coherent manner aimed at expanding mutually beneficial economic ties.

A new policy must more aggressively promote trade and investment and involve all relevant government agencies, while simultaneously strengthening our development assistance programs with those African countries demonstrating the strongest commitment to economic and political liberalization and poverty reduction. It must also promote the extinction of outstanding concessional bilateral debt and a more rapid application of the new debt reduction initiative of the World Bank and the International Monetary Fund (IMF). Finally, a new policy must include the payment of outstanding U.S. commitments to those international organizations whose programs are critical to progress in Africa, as well as a willingness to work to improve the performance of those organizations.

The Task Force calls on the president and the secretaries of state, commerce, and treasury, along with the U.S. trade representative and the administrator of USAID, to focus greater attention and provide stronger collective leadership on new initiatives that transform the nature and content of U.S. economic policies toward Africa. The Task Force calls upon members of Congress to provide the administration with the resources and support it will need to begin a new era of cooperation with an increasing number of African countries.

The Task Force is convinced that a new U.S. economic policy toward the countries of Africa should have as objectives the following:

- Increase U.S. two-way trade with African countries and American direct investment in Africa;

- Increase and strengthen U.S. development assistance in reforming countries to support sensible macroeconomic policies and to help create conditions that will attract even greater investment and produce greater trade;

- Improve debt reduction as an important tool for restoring the creditworthiness of African countries committed to economic and political liberalization and poverty reduction;

- Strengthen international cooperation in support of development in Africa.

AFRICA TODAY

Since the dawn of this decade, Africa has been experiencing profound social, political, and economic changes that are carrying

African countries into the new millennium with greatly improved prospects for economic development and growth. This renaissance is taking place amid equally dramatic changes in the global political economy and portends important opportunities for African nations to deepen their participation in the international system in numerous, mutually beneficial ways. The positive trends—democratization, economic reform, and settlement of long-standing conflicts—characterize the present era as the most promising period since the onset of African independence 40 years ago. While the continent's continuing problems should not be understated, it is evident that we are witnessing the inception of Africa's second independence.

A failure to fully appreciate the economic aspects of this continent-wide renewal and their bearing on Africa's security and political interests will result in lost opportunities to maximize and sustain positive change in ways benefiting not only African nations, but the United States and the larger global community as well. In terms of America's national interests, it should be self-evident that as we become more dependent on the expansion of world trade for our own economic well-being, the potential for significant growth in Africa—resulting in substantial new trade and investment opportunities at high rates of return—merits aggressive U.S. economic engagement with the continent.

U.S. ECONOMIC INTERESTS IN AFRICA

The United States has considerable interests in Africa's economic development. In an era of increasing international economic competition and rapid globalization, the United States should not neglect a region as enormous as Africa, with over 10 percent of the world's population and a wealth of untapped natural resources. Economic development in Africa will benefit the United States by producing stronger and larger emerging markets for U.S. exports and by enabling African nations to participate more in addressing problems that transcend national and regional boundaries, such as environmental degradation, international crime and terrorism, migration, and regional security matters. Sustainable development in Africa will also dramatically reduce the need for, and costs of, humanitarian assistance and intervention that have surpassed development assistance levels for Africa in too many recent years. As Africa grows and becomes more integrated into the global economy, trade and investment will completely replace official development assistance as the fuel for further economic expansion, ending the era of aid dependency.

The importance to the U.S. economy of expanding its exports is greater than ever before, as more than a third of economic growth in the United States now results from exports. Within another three years, more than 16 million jobs will depend upon overseas sales, and many American companies are already earning more than half their revenues abroad.

U.S. trade with Africa is already considerable. For example, in 1996, U.S. trade with the 12 countries of southern Africa totaled over $9 billion, a level comparable to trade with the 15 Republics of the former Soviet Union combined. Significantly, U.S. exports to Africa have grown over 20 percent a year in recent years. In 1995, U.S. businesses increased their exports to Sub-Saharan Africa by 23 percent to a total of $5.4 billion, and in 1996 that figure rose to $6.1 billion. Nevertheless, the U.S. market share in the region—at 6.7 percent—lags behind Japan's 7.2 percent and well behind the 30 percent share enjoyed by the European Union. Moreover, with imports from the region totaling $15.2 billion, the United States still runs a significant trade deficit, while most of our European allies maintain a trade surplus with the continent.

U.S. ECONOMIC POLICY TOWARD AFRICA

During the first four decades of Africa's independence from colonialism, American foreign policy toward the continent was overwhelmingly influenced by global competition between the United States and the former Soviet Union. Africa's economic development interests as well as American economic interests in Africa were largely marginalized because of the primacy of the Cold War. The end of the Cold War has led some policymakers to conclude incorrectly that there are no compelling reasons for continued U.S. economic engagement in Africa.[1]

Until recently, U.S. economic policy toward Africa has depended on the provision of aid as the principal instrument for advancing U.S. interests. Though subordinate to Cold War imperatives, development concerns have also been a part of the motivation for U.S. aid to Africa. Whereas in the 1960s, the focus was on "promoting growth," the 1970s witnessed a shift in emphasis to poverty reduction and meeting "basic human needs." During the 1980s, aid predominantly focused on support for "structural adjustment," or stabilization programs, and trade liberalization to encourage economic recovery and growth. In the 1990s, aid has since shifted to promote good governance and political democratization as a precondition for economic development.

More recently the Clinton administration has stated that the primary goal of U.S. economic policy toward Africa is to support sustainable development and to quicken the pace of that development, to boost U.S. trade and investment. In many ways, sustainable development embraces all the primary objectives of the preceding decades and represents a better and more integrated understanding of Africa's development challenges.

But regardless of the particular orientation of U.S. economic policy toward Africa over the years, its effectiveness has always suffered from the low priority it received within the prevailing foreign policy agenda and within the foreign policy bureaucracy.

Moreover, by limiting economic relations with Africa to those of aid-donor and aid-recipient, instead of promoting real partnerships utilizing a full range of aid, trade, investment, and debt management instruments, the United States wrongly casts Africa as a region of little economic significance or potential.

Frustrated by this legacy and cognizant of the economic dynamism

---

[1]Herman Cohen argues that while the Cold War certainly contributed to Africa's economic marginalization between 1975 and 1990, the main reason was failed African economic policies, which discouraged investments and production of wealth.

now manifesting itself on the continent, legislators recently introduced proposals in Congress that encourage reorienting U.S. economic policy by promoting American private-sector involvement in Africa and increasing the role of trade and investment as vehicles for supporting African economic development.

At the same time, proposals to restructure and reduce the U.S. foreign aid program raise serious questions about the future of U.S. aid to Africa (with the exception of Egypt). While economic assistance to Africa was regularly undercut by Cold War geostrategic and political issues, thereby retarding sustainable development, the post–Cold War period has been characterized by a sudden dismissal of development assistance on the grounds that it has achieved little positive development impact. This trend discounts the fact that efforts to reform aid and focus more on strengthening Africans' capacity to find their own development solutions are still in their infancy, and that aid has only recently been freed of its Cold War constraints. It also ignores the increased opportunities for more effective use of aid in countries that are implementing serious reform programs.

Unfortunately, the convergence of these developments (declining aid levels and increased interest in trade) has led to an often simplistic "trade versus aid" debate over which is the more constructive approach for changing U.S. economic policies toward Africa. Fortunately, efforts to avoid this false dichotomy are evidenced in the revised legislation.

With the recent reintroduction of the African Growth and Opportunity Act in Congress, and the upcoming G-7 economic summit in Denver—where new economic initiatives on Africa will figure prominently on the agenda—there exists a new momentum for redefining U.S. economic policy toward the continent. The administration is working to finalize proposals for a "Partnership for Economic Growth and Opportunity in Africa" that embraces most of the items proposed in the legislation. These developments, combined with U.S. support for the World Bank/IMF debt-reduction program for Heavily Indebted Poor Countries (HIPC), offer key components for what should become a more integrated U.S. economic policy toward Africa.

RECOMMENDATIONS

The Task Force is convinced that a new policy promoting economic relations with Africa must be driven more effectively by the White House than in the recent past, that it must strengthen the complementarity of development assistance programs and the new trade and investment initiatives, and that it must include new human and financial resource commitments to promote greater U.S. economic engagement in Africa. In addition, a new U.S. economic policy toward Africa necessitates both greater U.S. leadership in efforts to reduce Africa's unsustainable debt burden and payment by the United States of outstanding commitments to international organizations whose programs are critical to Africa's economic development.

Furthermore, to create an expanded economic partnership with the African continent of significant mutual benefit to both Americans and Africans, the president with the cooperation of Congress must broaden the proposed "Partnership for Economic Growth and Opportunity in Africa" program to include the following elements:

Trade and Investment

• Passage of an African Growth and Opportunity Act (which increases African access to U.S. markets, creates enterprise funds to mobilize greater American private-sector investment in Africa, increases the number of posts within key federal agencies concerned with U.S. economic policies toward Africa, creates a U.S.-Africa Economic Forum, and initiates planning for free trade agreements with African countries or groups of countries);

• Designation of one of the directors for African affairs at the National Security Council to be responsible for African economic affairs and the coordination of efforts under the "Partnership" program;

• More aggressive trade and investment promotion in Africa by the Export-Import Bank, OPIC, TDA, and the Commerce Department;

• New USDA efforts to utilize existing programs to increase agricultural trade with African countries and to help promote agro-business linkages through its trade-related programs in Africa.

The Task Force recognizes that the executive branch's draft "Partnership" program now includes most of the proposals contained in the legislation pending in the House of Representatives but believes that it is important to legislate these changes in U.S. economic policy toward Africa for several reasons. First, the legislation includes significant items absent from the administration's initiatives, specifically measures to increase African access to U.S. markets by eliminating trade barriers in the textile industry and increasing the Generalized System of Preferences (GSP) program benefits available to African exporters. Second, new statutory requirements on Africa policy are needed to change the mindset in the foreign affairs bureaucracy from donor to trade and development partner. Third, Congress similarly needs to debate this new approach in order to help enlighten members about the depth and breadth of U.S. economic interests in Africa. Finally, bipartisan support of this new U.S. economic policy toward Africa will send a positive signal to leaders in Africa and the rest of the world.

The Task Force also calls on the president to direct the agencies primarily responsible for trade and investment promotion—the Export-Import Bank, the Overseas Private Investment Corporation, and the Trade and Development Agency—along with the U.S. Agency for International Development, to coordinate efforts that facilitate the growth of the African private sector and to facilitate greater links between the American and African business communities. Similarly the Department of Commerce should commit larger numbers of Foreign Commercial Service officers to work in Africa and continue the post of minister counselor for southern Africa. The Task Force also believes that a major Department of Agriculture effort developing the agro-industry in Africa is long overdue. Similarly, the USDA should step up support for research, training, and technical assistance in Africa and promote agro-business linkages through its trade-related programs in Africa.

The Task Force also calls on the president to designate one of the directors for African affairs within the National Security Council to be responsible for dealing with aid, trade and investment, and debt reduction questions related to Africa.

Investments in Sustainable Development

- Appropriation of up to $1 billion a year for the next five years for the Development Fund for Africa and the African Development Foundation (with a portion of new funding to be made available to encourage greater regional cooperation and multi-country development projects);

- Removal of earmarks that reduce the administration's ability to flexibly promote development activities in a timely manner;

- Full funding for existing commitments to international organizations important to African development, including the International Development Association, the African Development Bank and Fund, and the United Nations.

The Task Force is convinced that there is a strong continuing role for bilateral development assistance to Africa and that current aid levels should be increased. Specifically, to reverse the decline in U.S. aid levels to Africa at a moment when it is more likely to be used more effectively than ever before, Congress should authorize and appropriate up to $1 billion for the Development Fund for Africa and the African Development Foundation in each of the next five years. The Task Force believes that while more emphasis is needed on promoting trade with Africa and U.S. private investment in Africa, the United States must expand its sustainable development programs to help reduce poverty, strengthen democratic governance and the rule of law, and invest in human resource development, all of which are necessary to help Africa create the economic base needed to meet global competition for export markets and investment funds, and to sustain economic growth.

The Task Force also recognizes the need for restructuring USAID to better perform in its development roles. It is worthwhile to consider a variety of alternative models such as a more decentralized and field-based institution with grant-making and auditing functions, and bilateral development finance institutions—such as the

United Kingdom's Commonwealth Development Corporation. However, any such restructuring should be considered in close collaboration with Congress and should not be allowed to weaken the content nor reduce the amount of bilateral aid going to Africa at this critical juncture.

Within both its development assistance programs and its new trade and investment initiatives, the administration must act on its commitment to support regional economic cooperation and integration in Africa by using a portion of development assistance funding to support multi-country development projects and encourage greater intra-African trade, investment, and private-sector development (beyond what USAID already has been doing in southern Africa). In both of its Trade and Development Policy reports, the administration has emphasized the need for African countries to accelerate efforts at regional economic integration in order to increase their appeal to potential investors by increasing their market size. Regional economic integration is also an important part of the process by which African economies become more active in the global economy.

The United States must also pay outstanding American commitments to the International Development Association, the African Development Bank and Fund, and the United Nations in order to carry a fair share of international cooperation in support of African development and to maintain leadership in shaping the global economy. These multilateral institutions are perhaps more important to Africa than any other world region. While the United States should push for reforms that improve the effectiveness of these institutions, the ability to do so requires the payment of outstanding obligations. Moreover, the arrears endanger important development resources for Africa and jeopardize the ability of U.S. firms to compete for projects financed by these institutions in African countries.

Debt Reduction

- A commitment to push for an accelerated, improved, and flexible implementation of the HIPC framework for debt relief in

Africa with an emphasis on restoring the creditworthiness of strongly reforming countries.[2]

The United States must continue to provide leadership that helps relieve Africa's unsustainable levels of debt. Africa's external debt is not large in absolute terms at $340 billion. The $199 billion owed by sub-Saharan nations is only one-third the amount owed by Latin America and half that owed by Europe and Central Asia or the Middle East. However, Africa's debt is exacerbated by the region's poverty and limited export income. Africa's debt burden is now almost as large as its total gross domestic product (GDP). This is, as Treasury Secretary Robert Rubin recently pointed out, "the result of a lot of mistakes made by too many countries and by too many lenders." Africa's heavy indebtedness discourages investors and dissuades private creditors from putting new money into the region, and discourages debtor governments from adopting painful economic reforms when their gains accrue mainly to foreign creditors. The cost of servicing foreign debt has a severe negative impact on a country's development by reducing funds for investing in the population's health and education and for importing inputs needed for development. The Task Force calls on the administration to press for a more rapid and effective implementation of the HIPC framework with certain significant amendments. The time frame for debt relief must be accelerated, the level of relief increased, and country coverage broadened. Specifically, the Task Force calls on the president to work with our G-7 allies to strengthen the HIPC debt reduction initiative as follows:

- The period of eligibility for multilateral debt reduction should be reduced from six years to three years;

---

[2] Because much of the data necessary to calculate estimates for debt reduction plans is held confidential by the World Bank and the IMF, no official figures for the cost of the HIPC proposals have been offered. However, a discussion of the complexities of estimating the costs of debt reduction proposals appears in the article by Jonathan E. Sanford in the attached *Background Materials* section. As Sanford notes, U.S. Secretary of Treasury Robert Rubin said in April 1996 that meeting the cost of reducing multilateral debt, "should be done with the resources, or at least predominantly with the resources, of the IMF and the World Bank. We do not think [it] should require contributions from the donor nations."

- The debt sustainability threshold ratios for debt service should be lowered to 15–20 percent and for debt-to-exports to 150–200 percent;

- Fiscal criteria should also be given greater weight for determining eligibility, and ceilings of between 15–20 percent should be set for the proportion of government revenue absorbed by debt repayments.

CONCLUSION

African renewal, as described earlier in this Statement, while largely self-generated, will nevertheless require significant international support and enhanced development cooperation if it is to be sustained. Such cooperation is equally important to the larger international community itself. The old notions of "aid donors" and "aid recipients" must give way to more relevant concepts that emphasize partnership and encompass the full range of areas of economic cooperation including trade and investment. Such international cooperation is equally necessary to address contemporary global concerns that transcend national and regional boundaries and affect the security and well-being of all nations. The quest for collective solutions to such global problems is greatly strengthened if participating nations have the economic strength and democratic forms of governance necessary to support resolutions that are sustainable.

While Africa's rebirth offers greater prospects for a new age of international cooperation with the continent, the current post–Cold War era is equally marked by the industrialized countries' turning away from much of the developing world, especially Africa.[3] This obviously shortsighted trend is not only lamentable, it is dangerous. Yet, absent the emergence of committed leadership from among these

---

[3] Michael Samuels argues that this statement is inaccurate and misleading. In his view, there have been many efforts by industrialized countries to expand economic activities with the developing world, such as the Asia Pacific Economic Cooperation (APEC) forum, suggestions for a Free Trade Area for the Americas (FTAA), as well as a number of new initiatives by the European Union and Japan and through the International Financial Institutions.

same economically developed democracies, the tendency toward narrow nationalism on their part will undermine Africa's opportunities to promote peace, democracy, and economic development. The need for a strong U.S. role in forging some manner of collective leadership in encouraging renewed international engagement in Africa is inescapable. As the world's sole remaining superpower, the leading Western nation without considerable colonial "baggage" on the continent, and a country where over 10 percent of the population is of African ancestry, the United States is uniquely situated to provide the impetus and the example for greater and mutually beneficial cooperation with Africa.

In the United States, the crumbling of the old conventions that sustained foreign policy throughout much of this century, and the need to redefine the national interests that will guide it into the future, should offer Africa new opportunities for greater engagement with the United States. There now exists a convergence of interests among African peoples' broad objectives of security, democracy, and economic development and the emerging U.S. framework for foreign policy in the 21st century.

Realistically, however, this moment of opportunity could easily be lost. Indeed, the low priority that continues to be given to African affairs by Washington despite this convergence, as well as the unchanged staple of negative stereotypes of Africa that continue to predominate in American attitudes toward Africa, are discouraging. These factors underline the need for new and innovative efforts to address the prevailing misperceptions of Africa's progress and of its importance to the United States and the global political economy as a whole.

The continent-wide renaissance in its fragile infancy, the opportunities offered by a redefinition of U.S. interests abroad, and the emergence of a new generation of African leaders suggest that the three years remaining in this century represent the best opportunity ever to end Africa's historic marginalization.

Unless the president provides the leadership needed to launch a new approach for U.S. policy toward Africa, it is unlikely that the various initiatives emanating from a scattering of federal agencies and Congress will provide a coherent vision or be very innovative and well integrated into our larger foreign policy agenda. Between now and the Denver Economic Summit, the president must decide that the African continent, with its 53 nations, nearly 800 million people, and enormous natural resources, is far too important to remain marginalized on the eve of a new century in which America will need a far more productive relationship with the continent than ever before. Such a relationship awaits Washington's new policy.

ENDORSERS OF THE STATEMENT

HAROLD M. AGNEW is the former Director of the Los Alamos Scientific Laboratory, President of General Atomics, Chairman of the General Advisory Committee to the Arms Control and Disarmament Agency (ACDA), and New Mexico State Senator. He is a member of the National Academy of Sciences.

KOFI APPENTENG* is a Partner in the law firm of Thacher Proffitt & Wood.

DAVID E. APTER is Henry J. Heinz II Professor of Comparative Political and Social Development at Yale University. He is Chairman of the Council on African Studies and Chairman of the Sociology Department.

JAMES E. BAKER* is an Adjunct Professor at Long Island University. He served as a Foreign Service Officer in the Department of State (1960–80) and as a senior official of the United Nations (1980–95).

PAULINE H. BAKER* is President of the Fund for Peace. She is also Co-Chair of the Women's Foreign Policy Group and teaches at Georgetown University. She served as Staff Director of the Senate African Affairs Subcommittee.

JOHN C. BEYER is President of Nathan Associates, an international economic consulting firm. He previously worked with the Ford Foundation and the Brookings Institution.

RICHARD E. BISSELL* was Assistant Administrator of the U.S. Agency for International Development between 1986 and 1993.

Note: Institutional affiliations are for identification purposes only.

*Individual is a member of the Independent Task Force on Promoting U.S. Economic Relations with Africa.

†Individual largely concurs with the Statement but submitted an additional view.

‡Individual participated in the Task Force discussions but chose to be an observer or was not asked to endorse the Statement because of his or her official capacity.

[18]

SALIH BOOKER* is Senior Fellow and Director for Africa Studies at the Council on Foreign Relations. He was a professional staff member of the House Foreign Affairs Committee, served in Africa as a Program Officer for the Ford Foundation, and worked as a consultant for the Carnegie Corporation, the U.N. Development Program (UNDP), and the African Development Foundation.

ZEB B. BRADFORD, JR., is Vice President of Military Affairs at the Traveler's Group. He was Chief of Plans and Programs for NATO/SHAPE headquarters in Belgium and headed International Strategic Planning for the United Technologies Corporation.

WILLIAM L. BRADLEY was an Associate Director of the Rockefeller Foundation and President of the Edward W. Hazen Foundation, prior to retirement.

LINDA P. BRADY is Chair of the Sam Nunn School of International Affairs at Georgia Tech. She worked on defense and arms control issues in the U.S. Departments of State and Defense during the Carter and Reagan administrations.

JOHN D. BREWER‡ is the Special Assistant to the Assistant Secretary of State for Intelligence and Research, Toby Gati. He was a Program Officer with the Woodrow Wilson Foundation and served on the staff of former U.S. Senator Wyche Fowler of Georgia.

ROBERT S. BROWNE* is President of the Twenty-First Century Foundation. He is the former U.S. Executive Director at the African Development Fund.

JUDITH BRUCE is the Director of the Gender, Family, and Development Program at the Population Council. She has written extensively on changing family roles, women's access to resources and their role on economic development, and the quality of reproductive health care.

THOMAS CALLAGHY is Chair of the Department of Political Science at the University of Pennsylvania and a member of the University's African Studies Center's Executive Committee.

HERMAN J. COHEN*† is Senior Adviser to the Global Coalition for Africa. He is a former Ambassador to Senegal and served as Assistant Secretary of State for Africa under George Bush.

ROBERTA COHEN is a Guest Scholar at the Brookings Institution. She is a former Deputy Assistant Secretary of State for Human Rights and a recipient of the USIA Superior Honor Award for reopening the public affairs program in Ethiopia.

JULIUS E. COLES* is the Director of Howard University's Ralph J. Bunche International Affairs Center. Prior to joining Howard University in 1994, he was a senior official with the U.S. Agency for International Development (USAID) for some 28 years and retired with the rank of Career Minister. He was Mission Director in Swaziland and Senegal and served in Vietnam, Morocco, Liberia, Nepal, and Washington, D.C.

GOODWIN COOKE is Professor of International Relations in the Maxwell School at Syracuse University. He was Ambassador to the Central African Republic.

CHESTER A. CROCKER is Distinguished Professor in the Practice of Diplomacy, Georgetown University, and Chairman of the Board at the U.S. Institute of Peace. He served as Assistant Secretary of State for African Affairs (1981–89).

KENNETH A. CUTSHAW is Counsel for the member-based law firm of Smith, Grambell and Russell. He served as Deputy and Acting Assistant Secretary of Commerce for Export Enforcement.

Note: Institutional affiliations are for identification purposes only.
*Individual is a member of the Independent Task Force on Promoting U.S. Economic Relations with Africa.
†Individual largely concurs with the Statement but submitted an additional view.
‡Individual participated in the Task Force discussions but chose to be an observer or was not asked to endorse the Statement because of his or her official capacity.

GEORGE A. DALLEY* is a Partner in the Law Office of Holland & Knight, practicing public and international law. He was Deputy Assistant Secretary of State for International Organizations and Congressional State Director.

MACEO N. DAVIS is Chairman and CEO of International Resources Exchange Corporation. He has done business in Africa and the Middle East for the past 15 years.

EDWIN A. DEAGLE, JR., is Chairman of the Potomac Finishing Company.

VIVIAN LOWERY DERRYCK* is a Senior Vice President and Director of Public Policy of the Academy for Educational Development and Senior Adviser to the Africa Leadership Forum. She also served as President of the African-American Institute and as Deputy Assistant Secretary of State in the Carter and Reagan administrations.

MUSTAFAH DHADA is Associate Professor of International Affairs at the School of International Affairs and Development at Clark Atlanta University. He is a recent Fulbright Scholar, specializing in conflict resolution and focusing on Lusophone Affairs.

JOEL DREYFUSS* is Editor-in-Chief of *Our World News*, a national weekly with a black perspective.

PEGGY DULANY* is Chair of ProVentures, a business development company for Latin America and southern Africa. She is also President and Founder of the Synergos Institute. She has consulted with the United Nations and the Ford Foundation on health care and family planning in Brazil, the United States, and Portugal, and with the National Endowment for the Arts on nonprofit management and planning.

JOSE W. FERNANDEZ* is a Partner at O'Melveny and Myers, LLP. He specializes in infrastructure projects in the developing world and has advised the governments of Ghana, Ivory Coast, Uganda, and Zambia on the restructuring and privatization of their telecommunications sectors.

FRANK E. FERRARI* is Vice President of ProVentures, Inc. He was Senior Vice President of the African-American Institute and the Director of the Institute's South African–Johannesburg Office.

DAVID J. FISCHER is President of the World Affairs Council of Northern California. A retired Ambassador, he served for nearly a decade in African Affairs in the U.S. Department of State.

WILLIAM R. FORD* is President of the African Development Foundation (ADF). He served in the U.S. Foreign Service for 20 years prior to joining ADF.

WAYNE FREDERICKS* was Deputy Assistant Secretary of State for Africa during the Kennedy and Johnson administrations. He was the head of the Africa and Middle East Program of the Ford Foundation (1967–74) and Executive Director of International Governmental Affairs of the Ford Motor Company (1974–88).

DENNIS GALLAGHER is the founder and Executive Director of the Refugee Policy Group.

ROBERT G. GARD is President of the Monterey Institute of International Studies. He was Director of the John Hopkins Bologna (Italy) Center and President of the National Defense University.

Note: Institutional affiliations are for identification purposes only.

*Individual is a member of the Independent Task Force on Promoting U.S. Economic Relations with Africa.

†Individual largely concurs with the Statement but submitted an additional view.

‡Individual participated in the Task Force discussions but chose to be an observer or was not asked to endorse the Statement because of his or her official capacity.

Endorsers of the Statement

HENRY LOUIS GATES, JR., is Chair of the Afro-American Studies
Department at Harvard University.

DAVID GINSBURG is currently Senior Counsel for the law firm of
Ginsburg, Feldman and Bress. He has served in the Roosevelt,
Truman, and Johnson administrations on domestic and foreign
affairs assignments.

TATIANA C. GFOELLER is Deputy Chief of Mission at the American Embassy, Ashgabat. She joined the U.S. Foreign Service in
1984.

DAVID F. GORDON* is Director of the U.S. Program at the Overseas Development Council.

ERNEST G. GREEN* is Managing Director of Public Finance at
Lehman Brothers.

BRANDON GROVE is Senior Consultant to the international public affairs firm of APCO Associates. A career Foreign Service Officer, he has served in West Africa and as Ambassador to Zaire.

ROBERT D. HAAS is the Chairman and Chief Executive Officer of
Levi Strauss and Company.

JOHN P. HALL is a corporate finance banker at JP Morgan focusing on the high-technology sector. He has worked and traveled
extensively in Africa.

CHARLES V. HAMILTON is Wallace S. Sayre Professor of Government at Columbia University.

ULRIC HAYNES, JR., is Executive Dean for International Relations
at Hofstra University. Formerly, he was an Administrative Officer in the U.N. Secretariat, a Foreign Service Officer, a member of the staff of the National Security Council, and U.S.
Ambassador to Algeria.

ELAINE HEIFETZ is a retired Foreign Service Reserve Officer who has served as a member of the U.S. Delegation to the United Nations and as Director of the U.S. State Department's New York Reception Center, which administered programs of distinguished international visitors.

HENRY L. HEINTZEN was a Foreign Service Officer in Ethiopia, Morocco, and Tanzania. He was also Chief of the Voice of America Africa Division and founding Director of the Voice of America program that trained thousands of foreign journalists.

JEAN HERSKOVITS* is Professor of African History at the State University of New York at Purchase. She has testified before Congress, served as a corporate and foundation consultant, and written about African affairs.

IRVIN HICKS, SR. is the former U.S. Ambassador to Ethiopia and Seychelles and Deputy U.S. Representative in the Security Council. He also served as Deputy Assistant Secretary of State for African Affairs.

CHRISTINE M. Y. HO* is President of Think, Inc., a global intelligence resource.

NANCY L. HOEPLI-PHALON is Editor-in-Chief of the Foreign Policy Association.

ADONIS E. HOFFMAN is an international lawyer and public policy counselor in Washington, D.C. A Senior Fellow at the World Policy Institute, he was Senior Associate at the Carnegie Endowment for International Peace and Director of African Affairs in the U.S. House of Representatives.

Note: Institutional affiliations are for identification purposes only.

*Individual is a member of the Independent Task Force on Promoting U.S. Economic Relations with Africa.

†Individual largely concurs with the Statement but submitted an additional view.

‡Individual participated in the Task Force discussions but chose to be an observer or was not asked to endorse the Statement because of his or her official capacity.

RICHARD O. HOPE is Vice President at the Woodrow Wilson National Fellowship Foundation. He was Executive Director of the QEM Project with the Carnegie Corporation and the Massachusetts Institute of Technology.

PARTICIA L. IRVIN is head of the Corporate Department and Managing Partner of the Washington, D.C., office of the law firm of Cooper, Liebowitz, Royster and Wright. She was Deputy Assitant Secretary of Defense in the Clinton adminstration and Partner in the Wall Street law firm of Milbank, Tweed, Hadley and McCloy.

ERIC K. JACKSON* is a Fellow in the Malcolm Wiener Center for Social Policy at the John F. Kennedy School of Government. His research focuses on the social impact of targeted investment strategies for development.

ROBERT D. JOFFE is a Partner at Cravath, Swaine and Moore, a member of both the Board of Directors and the Executive Committee of the Lawyers Committee for Human Rights, and a member of the Advisory Council of Human Rights Watch/Africa. He was in the Malawi Ministry of Justice on a Maxwell School Africa Public Service Fellowship (1967–69).

WILLARD R. JOHNSON* is Professor Emeritus of Political Science at the Massachusetts Institute of Technology, where he has specialized in African economic and political development and international relations.

RICHARD A. JOSEPH is Asa G. Candler Professor of Political Science of Emory University. He specializes in democratization and state building in Africa.

KENNETH I. JUSTER is a Partner in the law firm of Arnold and Porter. He was Acting Counselor of the U.S. Department of State (1992–93) and Deputy and Senior Adviser to the Deputy Secretary of State Lawrence Eagleburger (1989–92).

THOMAS G. KARIS is Senior Research Fellow at the Ralph Bunche Institute and Professor Emeritus of Political Science at the CUNY Graduate School.

ANDREW M. KARMARCK is retired from the World Bank, where he was successively Economic Adviser on Africa, Director of the Economics Department, and Director of the Economic Development Institute. He is the author of *The Economics of African Development* and *The Tropics and Economic Development.*

JORDAN KASSALOW is the Director of Onchocerciasis Programs for Helen Keller International. He is also a member of the Technical Consultative Committee for the World Bank's African Program for Onchocerciasis Control.

CHARLOTTE G. KEA‡ is a Senior Manager in the Eurasia division of Iridium, LLC. She is the former Special Assistant to the Assistant Secretary and Director General of the Commercial Service in the U.S. Department of Commerce.

EDMOND J. KELLER is Professor of Political Science and Director of the James S. Coleman African Studies Center at UCLA. He is a past President of the African Studies Association and a founding member of the Pacific Council on International Policy.

JOHN H. KELLY is Managing Director of International Equity Partners. He was Ambassador to Finland and to Lebanon and served as Assistant Secretary of State for the Near East and South Asia.

Note: Institutional affiliations are for identification purposes only.

*Individual is a member of the Independent Task Force on Promoting U.S. Economic Relations with Africa.

†Individual largely concurs with the Statement but submitted an additional view.

‡Individual participated in the Task Force discussions but chose to be an observer or was not asked to endorse the Statement because of his or her official capacity.

[26]

Endorsers of the Statement

HERBERT C. KELMAN is the Richard Clarke Cabot Professor of Social Ethics of Harvard University and directs the Program on International Conflict Analysis and Resolution at the Harvard Center for International Affairs. He received the 1997 Grawemeyer Award for Ideas Improving World Order.

ROBERT H. KNIGHT is Of Counsel to Shearmen and Sterling, of which he is former Senior Partner. He was Chairman of the Federal Reserve Bank of New York, General Deputy Assistant Secretary of Defense, and General Counsel of the U.S. Treasury Department.

LUCY KOMISAR is an international affairs journalist, a grantee of the John D. and Catherine T. MacArthur Foundation, and a Fellow of the John Simon Guggenheim Foundation, where she is writing a book on U.S. foreign policy and human rights in the 1970s and 1980s.

MAHESH K. KOTECHA* is a Managing Director of Capital Markets Assurance Corporation and CapMAC Asia. He is an Alternate Director of ASIA Ltd. and serves on the International Advisory Panel of the East African Development Bank. He was an investment banker with Kidder Peabody & Co. and a rating agency executive at Standard & Poor's.

STEPHEN E. LAMAR is the Vice President at Jefferson Waterman International. He has advised African governments on promoting trade and investment with the United States and served in the International Trade Administration's Office of Africa.

CAROL LANCASTER* is a Visiting Fellow at the Institute for International Economics and is on the faculty at the School of Foreign Service of Georgetown University. She formerly served as Deputy Administrator of the USAID and Deputy Assistant Secretary of State in the Bureau of African Affairs.

JAMES T. LANEY was U.S. Ambassador to the Republic of Korea (1993–97). He served as President of Emory University for 16 years.

JOHN FOSTER LEICH is a retired Foreign Service Officer, Divisional Director of Free Europe Committee, and Professor of Political Science and Foreign Languages. Currently, he is coordinator of Elderhostels, Institute of World Affairs in Salisbury, Connecticut.

LOUIS C. LENZEN is an attorney specializing in the mediation and arbitration of international commercial disputes.

WILLIAM M. LEOGRANDE is Professor of Government in the School of Public Affairs at American University. He served on the staff of the Democratic Policy Committee of the U.S. Senate.

DAVID F. LINOWES is Professor of Political Economy and Public Policy of the University of Illinois. He is former Chairman of the U.S. Privacy Protection Commission and Chairman of President Reagan's Commission on Privatization.

CHARLES MACCORMACK is President of Save the Children Federation, Inc., a development and humanitarian assistance organization working in 40 countries overseas and in the United States. He was President and CEO of World Learning/The Experiment in International Living.

JOHN D. MAGUIRE is President of Claremont Graduate University in California and a regional adviser of the Institute for International Studies. He has served as Provost at Wesleyan University, President of the State University of New York's College at Old Westbury, and adviser to the RAND Center for Research on Immigration Policy.

Note: Institutional affiliations are for identification purposes only.

*Individual is a member of the Independent Task Force on Promoting U.S. Economic Relations with Africa.

†Individual largely concurs with the Statement but submitted an additional view.

‡Individual participated in the Task Force discussions but chose to be an observer or was not asked to endorse the Statement because of his or her official capacity.

Endorsers of the Statement

ANTHONY MARX is Associate Professor of Political Science at Columbia University and a Guggenheim Fellow. He is the author of *Lessons of Struggle* and *Making Race and Nation.*

KENNETH MAXWELL is Nelson and David Rockefeller Senior Fellow for Inter-American Studies at the Council on Foreign Relations and former Director of Studies at the Council. He has written extensively on decolonization of the former Portuguese-speaking territories in Africa.

ROBERT C. MCFARLANE is President of McFarlane Associates, Inc.

MORA MCLEAN* is President of the African-American Institute. She served as Counsel to the Commerce Subcommittee of the U.S. House of Representatives and was the Ford Foundation's Representative for Nigeria and Assistant Representative for West Africa.

SHEILA AYRIN MCLEAN is President of the Association of Executive Search Consultants. She was General Counsel to the U.S. Government's Foreign Economic Assistance Agency and Senior Officer of the Ford Foundation and the Institute of International Education.

ROBERT S. MCNAMARA is former President of the World Bank.

ROBERT F. MEAGHER is Professor Emeritus of International Law at the Fletcher School of Law and Diplomacy. He has specialized in International Economic Law and Development in Africa and other Third World countries.

GWENDOLYN MIKELL* is Director of the African Studies Program in the School of Foreign Service at Georgetown University and the former President of the African Studies Association, U.S.A. She served as a Senior Fellow at the U.S. Institute of Peace and a Visiting Fellow at both the Institute for African Studies at the University of Ghana-Legon and the Institute for Social Research at the University of Natal in Durban, South Africa.

DAVID C. MILLER, JR., is the former U.S. Ambassador to Tanzania and Zimbabwe. He served as Special Assistant to the President for National Security Affairs (1989–90) and currently serves as President of the Corporate Council on Africa.

WANDRA G. MITCHELL* is Managing Director of Bahia Partners, Inc. She served as General Counsel for the USAID and prior to that was in private practice, specializing in antitrust and international trade law.

EDWIN S. MUNGER is Professor Emeritus of African Studies at the California Institute of Technology and President of the Cape of Good Hope Foundation.

HENRY R. NAN is Professor of Political Science and International Affairs at the Elliott School of International Affairs, the George Washington University. He served in the State Department (1975–77) and on the White House National Security Council (1981–83).

GABRIEL NEGATU* is Executive Director of the Forum of African Development Organizations (FADVO)–US, a consortium of African NGO Networks committed to U.S.-Africa relations.

PRISCILLA A. NEWMAN* is Vice President of AEA Investors, Inc. She previously worked as a staff member of the House Foreign Affairs Subcommittee on Africa and has worked in the area of international finance since that time.

DAVID D. NEWSOM is currently Cumming Professor of International Relations at the University of Virginia. He served as Assistant Secretary of State for Africa (1969–73) and Undersecretary for Political Affairs (1978–81).

Note: Institutional affiliations are for identification purposes only.
*Individual is a member of the Independent Task Force on Promoting U.S. Economic Relations with Africa.
†Individual largely concurs with the Statement but submitted an additional view.
‡Individual participated in the Task Force discussions but chose to be an observer or was not asked to endorse the Statement because of his or her official capacity.

[30]

Endorsers of the Statement

RICHARD F. PEDERSEN is a Board Member of the Center for Civic Education. He was Counselor of the State Department, U.S. Ambassador to Hungary, Deputy U.S. Representative to the U.N. Security Council, and President of the American University in Cairo.

ROBERT PELLETREAU is a Partner in the international law firm of Afridi and Angell with offices in New York, Washington, D.C., the U.A.E., and Pakistan. He served in the U.S. Department of State as Assistant Secretary for Near Eastern Affairs and as Ambassador to Egypt, Tunisia, and Bahrain.

GERARD PIEL was President and Publisher of *Scientific American* (1948–86).

GUSTAV RANIS is the Frank Altschul Professor of International Economics at Yale University and the Director of the Yale Center for International and Area Studies. He was Assistant Administrator for Program and Policy at USAID and Director of the Yale Economic Growth Center.

OGDEN REID is President of the Council of American Ambassadors and a member of several corporate boards, including Patent Development Corporation, General Physics, and Royce Labs. He served as the U.S. Ambassador to Israel (1959–61) and as a member of Congress (1961–74) from the state of New York.

YOLONDA C. RICHARDSON* is Program Officer at the Carnegie Corporation of New York working in the area of women's health and development and transitions to democracy in Africa. She serves on the board of several national public interest organizations and is a member of the American and National Bar Association, the Association of Black Foundations Executives, and the American Public Health Association.

JOHN J. ROBERTS is Vice Chairman–External Affairs of American International Group, Inc., an extensive worldwide network of insurance and financial services organizations in 130 countries and jurisdictions. He was Executive Vice President–Foreign General of American International Group, Inc.

RIORDAN ROETT is Sarita and Don Johnston Professor of International Relations and Director of the Latin American Studies Program at the Johns Hopkins Nitze School of Advanced International Studies (SAIS).

LEONARD H. ROBINSON* is a Fellow at the McCormack Institute of Public Affairs, University of Massachusetts–Boston and President of LHR International, a policy consulting firm. He was Deputy Assistant Secretary of State and the first President of the African Development Foundation.

PATRICIA L. ROSENFIELD* is Chair of the Carnegie Corporation of New York's Program on Strengthening Human Resources in Developing Countries. Prior to joining Carnegie, Dr. Rosenfield established, and for nine years ran, the Social and Economic Research Component of the UNDP/World Bank/World Health Organization Special Program for Research and Training in Tropical Diseases.

CAROL KNUTH SAKOIAN* is Director of International Business Development for Scholastic, Inc. She has worked in many countries throughout Africa.

Note: Institutional affiliations are for identification purposes only.

*Individual is a member of the Independent Task Force on Promoting U.S. Economic Relations with Africa.

†Individual largely concurs with the Statement but submitted an additional view.

‡Individual participated in the Task Force discussions but chose to be an observer or was not asked to endorse the Statement because of his or her official capacity.

Endorsers of the Statement

MICHAEL A. SAMUELS*† is founder and president of Samuels International Associates, Inc., an international business and policy consulting firm. He has served as Ambassador to the General Agreement on Tariffs and Trade (GATT), Deputy U.S. Trade Representative, and U.S. Ambassador to Sierra Leone.

FRANK SAVAGE* is Chairman of Alliance Capital Management International and a member of the Board of Directors of Alliance Capital Management Corporation. He was Senior Vice President of the Equitable Life Assurance Society and Chairman of Equitable Capital Management Corporation.

OSCAR SCHACHTER is Hamilton Fish Professor Emeritus of International Law and Diplomacy at Columbia School of Law.

DANIEL A. SHARP* is President and CEO of the American Assembly of Columbia University, whose most recent program was on U.S. national interests and Africa. He has held leadership positions in the United States and state government, private industry, not-for-profits and universities.

SALLY SWING SHELLEY is the Radio Correspondent at the United Nations for Associated Press Special Assignment and Maryknoll Catholic Radio. She was a Director in the U.N. Department of Public Information, serving as an election supervisor in Namibia and as head of the Nongovernmental Section.

JAMES R. SILKENAT is a Partner at Winthrop, Stimson, Putnam and Roberts in New York. He is a former Chairman of the American Bar Association Section of International Law and Practice and regularly works on project finance and privatization matters in Africa.

JOSEPH J. SISCO is a Partner in the international management consulting firm Sisco Associates and a Director of Braun, International Public Group Inc., Government Services, Inc., Raytheon, and the Newport News Shipbuilding. He is the former U.S. Undersecretary of State and President of American University.

THEODORE C. SORENSEN is a Senior Partner at Paul, Weiss, Rifkind, Wharton, and Garrison and a member of the Board of the Council on Foreign Relations. He was Special Counsel to President John F. Kennedy.

PAUL SOROS is on the Advisory Board of Quantum Industrial Holdings and a director of numerous corporations. Formerly, he served as CEO of Soros Associates, an international engineering company.

SCOTT M. SPANGLER* is a former Assistant Administrator of USAID. He is currently a private investor in Phoenix, Arizona.

JOHN STREMLAU* is Staff Adviser to the Council on Preventing Deadly Conflict at the Carnegie Endowment for International Peace. He was Deputy Director of Policy Planning at the U.S. Department of State (1989–94).

JACK B. SUNDERLAND is President of American Independent Oil Company. He has been active in business in Africa and the Near East since 1961.

JAMES S. SUTTERLIN is Distinguished Fellow in U.N. Studies at Yale University and Adjunct Professor of Political Science at Long Island University. He is the former Director of the Executive Office of the U.N. Secretary-General and served as Inspector-General of the U.S. Foreign Service.

FRANCIS X. SUTTON is former Deputy Vice President (International) at the Ford Foundation. He is currently a consultant to Aga Khan University and a writer on foundations and development.

Note: Institutional affiliations are for identification purposes only.

*Individual is a member of the Independent Task Force on Promoting U.S. Economic Relations with Africa.

†Individual largely concurs with the Statement but submitted an additional view.

‡Individual participated in the Task Force discussions but chose to be an observer or was not asked to endorse the Statement because of his or her official capacity.

Endorsers of the Statement

RUSSELL E. TRAIN is Chairman Emeritus of the World Wildlife Fund. He is a former Administrator of the Environmental Protection Agency (1973–77), Chairman of the Council on Environmental Quality (1970–73), and Undersecretary of Interior (1969–79). He founded the African Wildlife Leadership Foundation in 1961.

J. MICHAEL TURNER* is Associate Professor of African and Latin American history at Hunter College–City University of New York. He was the Democracy/Governance Adviser for USAID in Mozambique, a Project Manager for the Democratic Initiatives Project, and a Program Officer initiating the Ford Foundation's Afro-Brazilian Affairs program in Rio. He has worked as a consultant for United Support of Artists for Africa, the World Bank, and the U.N. Secretariat.

MICHAEL H. VAN DUSEN is the Democratic Chief of Staff on the Committee on International Relations in the House of Representatives.

MICHAELA WALSH is President of Women's Asset Management, Inc. She is a member of the Board of Directors of Women's World Banking and the Zimbabwe Progress Fund, among others.

CARL WARE is Senior Vice President and President, Africa Group, the Coca-Cola Company. He serves as Chairman of the Board of Trustees of Clark Atlanta University and is a board member of the Southern Africa Enterprise Development Fund, the African-American Institute, and the Governor's Development Council (Georgia).

CHERRI D. WATERS* is Vice President of InterAction, a coalition of over 150 U.S.-based relief and development agencies. She was Senior Director for Policy and Research for the National Summit on Africa, Executive Director of the TransAfrica Forum Policy Institute, and Director of the Office of Learning and Dissemination at the African Development Foundation.

LOUIS T. WELLS is the Herbert F. Johnson Professor of International Management at Harvard Business School.

CHARLES W. WHALEN, JR., is Vice President of the Washington Institute of Foreign Affairs. He was a House member in Congress and served for six years on the Subcommittee on African Affairs.

C. S. WHITAKER is University Professor (Emeritus in Political Science and Anthropology) at the University of Southern California and Senior Fellow at the James S. Coleman African Studies Center, University of California, Los Angeles. He is a former Dean of Social Sciences at the University of Southern California.

JENNIFER SEYMOUR WHITAKER* is Deputy National Director and Senior Fellow of the Council on Foreign Relations and former Co-Director of the Committee on African Development Strategies. She is the author of *How Can Africa Survive?* and *Salvaging the Land of Plenty.*

IRVING A. WILLIAMSON‡ is Deputy General Counsel in the Office of the U.S. Trade Representative.

ERNEST J. WILSON III* is Director of the Center for International Development and Conflict Management and Professor of Government and Politics at the University of Maryland, College Park. He was Director for International Programs and Resources on the National Security Council.

Note: Institutional affiliations are for identification purposes only.

*Individual is a member of the Independent Task Force on Promoting U.S. Economic Relations with Africa.

†Individual largely concurs with the Statement but submitted an additional view.

‡Individual participated in the Task Force discussions but chose to be an observer or was not asked to endorse the Statement because of his or her official capacity.

Endorsers of the Statement

LUCY WILSON BENSON is President of Benson Associates, political and international consultants. She was Undersecretary of State for International Security, Science, and Technology and serves on several corporate, foundation, and nonprofit international relations boards.

W. HOWARD WRIGGINS is a retired Professor of International Politics at Columbia University. He is a former member of the Policy Planning Council at the U.S. Department of State, member of the National Security Council Staff, and Ambassador to Sri Lanka.

ANDREW J. YOUNG is Co-Chairman of GoodWorks International and is the former U.S. Ambassador to the United Nations.

GEORGE H. YOUNG III* is Managing Director in the Telecommunications Group at Lehman Brothers, Inc.

ARISTIDE R. ZOLBERG is University-in-Exile Professor of Political Science at the New School for Social Research. He has published widely on Africa and Europe and on international migration and refugees.

Rapporteur

MARILYN R. GAYTON is Research Associate for the Africa Studies Program at the Council on Foreign Relations.

Background Materials

THEODROS DAGNE

"AFRICA: TRADE AND DEVELOPMENT INITIATIVES BY THE CLINTON ADMINISTRATION AND CONGRESS"

Congressional Research Service, April 28, 1997

SUMMARY

In February 1997, the Clinton administration submitted the second of five annual reports on the administration's Comprehensive Trade and Development Policy for Africa as required by section 134 of the Uruguay Round Agreements Act (House Document 103–3415, Vol. 1.). The report outlines the administration's primary goals on trade-related issues and proposes several new initiatives on trade and investment. On April 24, 1997, members of the African Trade and Investment Caucus introduced a bill, H.R. 1432, on U.S.-Africa trade and investment issues. Administration officials say they support most of the recommendations in the bill and will work with Congress to address some concerns.

INTRODUCTION[1]

Beginning in 1994, interest in trade and investment issues related to Africa began to increase, reflecting concerns over the impact of the Uruguay Round Agreements Act on Africa. In 1994, Congress called on the President to submit a report on trade and development policy toward Africa. The first report was submitted by the President in February 1996. The President's second report gives an

---

[1] For background on the first President's report, see CRS Report 96–639 by Theodros Dagne.

overview of progress made by some African countries and provides critical assessment of where reforms are needed. Reaction to the President's two reports has been mixed. Some critics of the first report, however, say they were encouraged by the administration's efforts reflected in the second report. Shortly after the first report was issued in February 1996, several members of Congress formed a bipartisan congressional African Trade and Investment Caucus to "review the President's policy document and to initiate a broader discussion." In September 1996, several members of the caucus introduced legislation, entitled African Growth and Opportunity: End of Dependency Act of 1996, to establish a new trade and investment policy toward Africa. The bill died in committee in the 104th Congress. A revised version of last year's bill (H.R. 1432) was introduced on April 24, 1997, by several members of the African Trade Caucus.

THE PRESIDENT'S REPORT[2]

Africa's economic success and stability contribute directly to "the national and economic security of the United States," according to the President's report. The administration makes the case that Africa is economically important, with 10 percent of the world's population and untapped natural resources. This view, according to some observers, counters the widely held opinion that Africa is a "basket case" and has no strategic significance to the United States. The report notes significant increases in U.S. exports to sub-Saharan Africa, with an estimated $5.4 billion in 1995. But the report acknowledges that U.S. market share is still negligible compared with the European Union, which has an estimated 30 percent of the market, while the U.S. share is estimated at 6–7 percent—equal to that of Japan.

Africa's significance as a trade partner is highlighted in the report as compared with other regions. The report states that U.S. exports to sub-Saharan Africa exceed exports to all countries of the former Soviet Union combined, while exports to South Africa

---

[2] A Comprehensive Trade and Development Policy for the Countries of Africa. A report submitted by the President of the United States to the Congress, February 18, 1997.

alone surpass exports to Eastern Europe. While the U.S. trade deficit with sub-Saharan Africa ($6.6 billion in 1995) is high because of oil imports, the report reflects optimism that the deficit may be reduced once American businesses learn more about the profitability of trade with Africa. The report states that with the end of conflicts in parts of Africa and progress in democratization, as well as wide economic reforms and trade liberalization, prospects for increased investment look good.

The report provides data on the economic performances of sub-Saharan African countries. An estimated 30 countries have carried out economic reforms of their economies with the support of the IMF and the World Bank. Moreover, "multilateral trade liberalization and preferential programs have greatly reduced, though not eliminated, the trade barriers faced by sub-Saharan merchandise goods and service exports to the United States and other countries." The report suggests increased investment in the "30 fast-growing" countries in sub-Saharan Africa with an estimated real growth rate of 11–12 percent. While nonreform-oriented countries, such as Nigeria and Angola, showed positive growth in Gross Domestic Product (GDP) in large part owing to their oil wealth, crisis-prone countries such as Zaire, Liberia, and Burundi had declining or negative growth.

The report acknowledges that privatization in many African countries has been slow in part because of fear of higher unemployment and lack of capital. African governments are concerned that privatization would deny them the resources necessary to fulfill social obligations to the vast poverty-stricken populations. One approach being pursued by African governments, according to the President's report, is to maintain a minority share in privatized companies. African countries have made important strides in regional economic integration. The report cites recent trade protocols signed by member countries of the Southern African Development Community (SADC) and refers to the efforts of the West African Economic and Monetary Union (WAEMU). The report states the administration's intent to support regional integration but falls short in specifics. Although the President's first report sought to put heavy emphasis on regional integration as a tool for increased trade and investment, the second report deemphasizes this approach, reflecting a lack of progress among African states in this area.

The President's report outlines U.S. trade and development policy toward Africa and identifies four strategic objectives: "1) increasing trade flows between the United States and sub-Saharan Africa; 2) promoting economic reform as well as the development of the private sector and infrastructure; 3) improving the investment climate; and 4) strengthening moves toward democratic governance." The administration intends to further these strategic objectives by employing current initiatives and by introducing new ones. Despite clarity in strategic objectives, the administration's implementation approaches appear vague and lack substantial resources. Tools cited by the administration include "bilateral technical and development assistance, increased government-to-government dialogue, export promotion, and trade facilitation programs."

Despite progress and important gains in many African countries, the report stresses, additional reforms are necessary to maintain sustainable growth. Macroeconomic stabilization, sustained structural reforms, increased private savings, removal of restrictive investment policies, developing the private sector, and improving infrastructure are key to sustainable development in Africa.

NEW INITIATIVES

The President's report proposes several new initiatives to promote African development through increased trade and investment.

Economic Reform
- The Department of the Treasury will continue to provide strong backing to the World Bank/IMF/Paris Club for the debt-reduction initiative started after the 1995 G-7 Halifax Summit to assist heavily indebted poor countries (HIPCs).

- The administration (Treasury, State, NEC, USAID) will be working with the United Nations, International Monetary Fund, World Bank, and World Trade Organization to develop more Africa-specific proposals in time for consideration at the next G-7 Summit in Denver in July, 1997.

Trade Liberalization and Promotion
- The Deputy United States Trade Representative (USTR) has in the past year assumed responsibility for senior-level direction of U.S. trade relations with Africa. In addition, USTR is considering creation of an Assistant USTR to deal with trade policy questions related to Africa.

- The Commerce Department will work with the private sector to post a Home Page for African Opportunities on the Internet that will include information on trade and investment opportunities, trade programs, equity funds, and banks available for trade and project finance.

Investment Liberalization
- Five Overseas Private Investment Corporation (OPIC) funds are available to invest equity in projects in Africa, including a $300 million fund that will focus on private, water-related projects.

- The administration strongly supports the "Reach Initiative," a new $40 million IFC program to extend its work to developing countries in which there has been little interest on the part of world capital markets and where IFC itself has not been active.

Private-Sector Development
- Eximbank will identify markets in which it currently is not open for routine transactions.

- The Department of Labor will work to help improve the ability of labor ministries to enhance labor-market information capabilities, strengthen labor standards and training, and enforce laws.

Infrastructure Enhancement
- The administration will establish an interagency group on private infrastructure promotion and finance for Africa.

- The Energy Department will develop a framework for a sustainable U.S. energy policy vis-à-vis Africa.

Promoting U.S. Economic Relations with Africa

ANALYSIS

The President's second trade report offers 63 initiatives on trade- and investment-related issues—but many of these, critics claim, represent only limited changes from previous proposals. The second report is limited in scope in part because of disagreements within the administration and pressure to meet congressional deadlines to submit the report, observers believe. Nonetheless, administration officials point to some accomplishments in efforts to promote trade and investment, in part through USAID's Greater Horn of Africa Initiative, development programs, and the Southern Africa Initiative (SAI). While observers credit the administration for assisting Horn of Africa leaders in their efforts to restructure and revitalize the Inter-Governmental Authority for Development (IGAD), critics note that the program was minimally funded and had limited impact on the private sector or increased trade.

The President's report states that the recently authorized $120 million private investment fund by OPIC for projects in sub-Saharan Africa is an important initiative. Concerning debt relief, the report states that the administration will continue to back the IMF, World Bank, and the Paris Club on a debt-reduction initiative adopted at the 1995 G-7 Halifax Summit to assist heavily indebted poor countries (HIPCs). Many observers regard the Halifax initiative as an important effort on the part of donor countries, since it seeks to assist HIPCs to reduce debt and not just refinance. A recent statement by NGO groups states that "the HIPC initiative for debt relief, although limited in scope, the HIPC framework constitutes a breakthrough."[3] Among other things the initiative coordinates the initiatives of all creditors. Despite this praise, however, critics argue that the second report places heavy emphasis on traditional development strategies and repackages ongoing programs as new ones. There is no infusion of "new money" to some of the proposed new initiatives; instead, the report relies on existing funds or policy statements.

---

[3] American NGO Policy Statement for the Denver G-7 Summit, March 26, 1997.

OVERVIEW OF H.R. 1432,
AFRICAN GROWTH AND OPPORTUNITY ACT

Disappointed by the President's first report, members of the African Trade Caucus began to develop their own initiative in mid-1996. On April 24, 1997, several members of the African Trade Caucus introduced a 36-page bill calling for drastic change in U.S.-Africa trade relations. The bill emphasizes economic self-reliance through expanded private-sector activities, increased trade and investment, elimination of trade barriers, and focusing on countries committed to economic reform. The bill provides additional flexibility to the President under the Development Fund for Africa (DFA) through waiver authority of congressional set asides. However, the bill excludes set-aside programs such as child survival activities, immunization programs, health and nutrition programs, HIV/AIDS, and basic education. While this bill retained provisions introduced in the last Congress, several new additions are included, and some aspects of the current bill seem accommodating to concerns raised by private groups and the administration.

One change is the source and amount of the proposed equity and infrastructure funds. These funds would be used to "achieve long-term capital appreciation" and to encourage investments in infrastructure projects. Previously, the bill authorized $30 million each for the two funds, while the $650 million proposal for the two funds in the current bill calls on OPIC to "exercise the authorities it has" to establish these funds. The proposed $150 million equity fund and the $500 million infrastructure fund would be managed by professional "private fund managers" but monitored by the OPIC. Capital for the funds is expected to come from a combination of sources, including private equity capital and OPIC guaranteed debt.

The bill places considerable emphasis on women entrepreneurs, debt relief, sustainable development, and approaches championed by advocates of grassroots development. The absence of such wording was a contentious aspect of the previous bill.

Some provisions, such as the creation of a United States–Sub-Saharan Africa Trade and Economic Cooperation Forum, have been strengthened in the current bill by abandoning the "sense of Congress" language from the previous bill and changing "should" to "shall." The bill would establish a Forum with the objective of convening annual high-level meetings between senior U.S. and African officials to discuss wide-ranging issues in the economic sphere. Specifically, the bill directs the President to instruct the Secretaries of Treasury, State, Commerce, and the United States Trade Representative (USTR) to meet annually with their counterparts in Africa who are committed to reforms. Participation of the NGO community and private groups is also encouraged. In addition, the bill calls on the President to meet once every two years with African heads of state who are committed to economic reform.

The bill calls for the establishment of a Free Trade Area between the United States and sub-Saharan countries and directs the administration to prepare a detailed plan for this and report to Congress not later than one year after enactment. The bill would add board members with private-sector background in sub-Saharan Africa to OPIC and the Export-Import Bank. The bill would also create a position for an Assistant United States Trade Representative (USTR) for Africa in the office of the USTR.

POLICY DEBATE

After several months of debate between members of the Caucus and administration officials, and mounting pressure on the administration, in mid-April 1997, the Clinton administration submitted a new draft proposal to congressional staff. The administration's new proposal shows important shifts in policy and incorporates most of the trade legislation recommendations. It proposes to enhance market access to General System of Preferences (GSP)—eligible and less-developed countries (LDCs).

The new administration initiative, which has not yet been made public, reportedly proposes to fund the equity and infrastructure funds under OPIC direction with an estimated capital of $650 million. It also proposes to appoint an Assistant USTR for Africa and a senior official of EXIM Bank to advise the Board of Directors; and it supports the establishment of a cabinet-level U.S.-Africa Economic Forum.

In what the administration refers to as Level Three Participation, negotiations on free trade agreements with high-performing, growth-oriented countries would be pursued. There are areas of disagreement between the administration and congressional negotiators over this new proposal, however, and the administration is concerned about aspects of the recently introduced African Growth bill. Of particular concern is the reauthorization of GSP for Africa separately. Administration officials also hoped for a "Sense of Congress" instead of a bill, which was rejected by congressional negotiators. Senior administration officials say they will not oppose the bill but would suggest modifications after the bill is introduced.[4]

Many Africa watchers appear encouraged by the increased level of interest in Congress on expanding trade and investment with Africa. Dozens of African ambassadors in Washington and senior officials of African governments formally endorsed last year's African Trade Caucus initiative on Africa. Some critics contend, however, that the bill is too detailed and ambitious, and its chances of passage limited. One important initiative in the bill is the authority given to the President to remove earmarks from the DFA to provide greater flexibility in program design and implementation. But since the bill protects several programs, the President's flexibility is limited. Administration officials argue that some language in the bill, such as that directing the President to instruct his cabinet members to meet with foreign officials, raises constitutional issues. Congressional sources dismiss this argument, saying that there are precedents.

---

[4] Briefing by senior administration official at the National Security Council, April 24, 1997.

RAYMOND W. COPSON

"AFRICA: U.S. FOREIGN ASSISTANCE ISSUES"

Congressional Research Service, July 29, 1997

SUMMARY

Legislative efforts to restructure the U.S. foreign assistance program have resulted in substantial reductions in aid to Africa, although the cuts have been somewhat less than anticipated at the outset of the 104th Congress. The actual appropriation under the Development Fund for Africa (DFA) is estimated at $665 million in FY1997, compared to levels of over $800 million earlier in the decade. Reductions in indirect aid due to cuts in contributions to the World Bank's International Development Association (IDA) have not had an immediate impact on IDA lending to Africa. Analysts anticipate long-term consequences, however, if U.S. reductions continue.

Proponents of reducing aid to Africa initially argued that the United States has few interests there now that the Cold War is over and should focus on regions of greater geo-political and economic relevance. This position seemed to moderate as the debate went forward, and congressional reports and bills acknowledged U.S. humanitarian, economic, and other interests in Africa. But reductions were made nonetheless, as part of the effort to reduce the overall U.S. budget deficit.

Opponents of reductions argue that the United States has unique, historic responsibilities in Africa. They also maintain that cuts are jeopardizing recent African progress toward free-market and democratic reforms, potentially creating costly long-term problems. Proponents of aid emphasize what they see as significant economic interests in Africa, which Brian Atwood, Administrator of the U.S. Agency for International Development (USAID), has described as a potentially important emerging market. Supporters of Africa aid want to maintain special earmarks for Africa programs, fearing that a future Administration might reduce Africa's aid levels in favor of other regions and programs. Others view the earmarks as an undue constraint on executive-branch flexibility.

U.S. assistance finds its way to Africa through a variety of channels, including the USAID-administered Development Fund for Africa (DFA), food aid programs, and indirect aid provided through international organizations. Overall U.S. assistance through all channels probably totaled just over $2 billion in FY1996. The United States has traditionally been the second-leading development aid donor to sub-Saharan Africa after France, but fell to fourth place— behind France, Japan, and Germany—in 1995. The United States devotes a much smaller portion of its aid to the region than most other western donors.

U.S. assistance to sub-Saharan Africa reached a peak in 1985, when global competition with the Soviet Union was at a high point. As the Cold War eased, security assistance programs for Africa began to drop. To counter falling aid levels, Congress created the DFA, which was earmarked at over $800 million before FY1996, when the earmark was dropped in favor of proportionality formulas intended to protect Africa's aid levels relative to other regions. Bilateral economic assistance for Africa today is close to the FY1990 low.

The Clinton Administration, like its predecessor, is pushing African recipients for economic and democratic reforms, while placing increased emphasis on population and environmental programs. It has launched special initiatives on southern Africa and the Horn, and pledged $600 million over three years to assist South Africa in its post-apartheid transition. U.S. assistance also supports African conflict resolution programs.

MOST RECENT DEVELOPMENTS

S. 955, the Foreign Operations Appropriation, passed the Senate on July 17, 1997, and does not include an earmark for the Development

Fund for Africa. Report language directs that no funds be made available for the Administration's proposed African Crisis Response Force (see Legislation section below for further details).

The House version of the Foreign Operations Appropriation has been reported and is awaiting a bill number. While the bill does not earmark DFA, report language states an expectation that a "significant portion" of the resources provided for Child Survival programs and Development Assistance will be committed to Africa. This bill earmarks $11.5 million for African Development Foundation, and $25 million for the African Development Fund, "soft-loan" window of the African Development Bank. The bill prohibits Foreign Military Financing for Sudan and Liberia and requires notification of Committees on Appropriations of aid to Liberia, Sudan, and Congo (Kinshasa). The report accompanying the bill supports the Administration's Greater Horn of Africa Initiative but seeks more information on a proposed food security initiative. The report directs USAID to use development assistance and disaster assistance funds for capacity building in areas of southern Sudan outside government control; notes serious human rights violations in Kenya; supports the Administration African Crisis Response Initiative; strongly recommends that U.S. representatives at IFIs oppose lending to Nigeria; and for Liberia, waives prohibitions on aid to countries in default on past U.S. loans.

BACKGROUND AND ANALYSIS

At the beginning of the 104th Congress, proposals to restructure and reduce the U.S. foreign assistance program raised questions about the future of U.S. aid to sub-Saharan Africa. Many questioned the strategic rationale for assisting Africa in the post-Cold War era, and asserted that thirty years of U.S. assistance had accomplished little—whether in terms of promoting economic growth and democratization, or achieving other objectives. The critics generally favored continuing humanitarian assistance in response to African famine and other disasters, but sought sharp cuts or a termination of efforts to accomplish other objectives.

Moves to reduce aid to Africa were strenuously opposed by
organizations and individuals that had sought over many years not
only to increase the level of U.S. economic assistance to the region,
but more generally to raise Africa to a higher priority on the U.S.
foreign policy agenda. They rejected the view that Africa is of little or no interest to the United States and insisted that historic and
cultural ties gave the United States a unique responsibility for
assisting Africa. Some maintained that cuts in aid would only
worsen grave African problems that would have to be faced in the
future at greater expense. Brian Atwood, Administrator of the
U.S. Agency for International Development (USAID), also maintained that the United States had important economic interests in
Africa that were not well recognized (see below).

As the aid debate proceeded during 1995, it became apparent that
cuts for Africa would be somewhat less than many had initially anticipated. The view that the United States has important humanitarian, economic, and other objectives in Africa came to be reflected
in report language on the major foreign assistance bills, and in the
bills themselves. Nonetheless, many continued to insist that in the
interest of reducing the U.S. budget deficit, assistance programs for
Africa, like other programs, had to be substantially cut—and substantial cuts were eventually imposed.

The FY1996 Foreign Operations appropriation (P.L. 104-107) did
not include a specific earmark for the Development Fund for Africa
(DFA), which is the principal bilateral aid channel for the sub-Saharan region. Nonetheless, it did fund a global development assistance
program and set a proportionality formula that provided somewhat
more for Africa than bills appearing at the beginning of the 1995.
The formula stated that the President "shall seek to assure" that Africa
receives "substantially the same proportion" of aid as in the previous year, leading to an initial calculation that the DFA would total
about $675 million. USAID officials now estimate that the DFA for
FY1996 was between $665 million and $675 million. Aid to Africa
in FY1997 is provided under the Omnibus Consolidated Appropriations
bill (P.L. 104-208), which also includes a proportionality formula that
could yield a DFA of $679 million. Current Administration esti-
mates, however, place the figure somewhat lower (Table 1).

Table 1. Development Fund for Africa, Requests and Appropriations

($millions)

	FY1994	FY1995	FY1996	FY1997 (est.)	FY1998 (request)
Request	800.0	863.6	802.1	704.0	700.0
Actual appropriation	784.0	802.0	665.0–675.0	665.1	

U.S. Aid to Africa: An Overview

U.S. assistance finds its way to Africa through a variety of channels. Bilateral or country-to-country aid, also sometimes known as direct assistance, is given by the U.S. Government to African governments and their agencies or to non-governmental organizations (NGOs) or private and voluntary organizations (PVOs) working within the host country. Multilateral aid, or indirect assistance, is given first to international financial institutions (IFIs) and U.N. agencies, which in turn channel it to Africa through their own programs.

Bilateral Aid. Bilateral aid obligations to sub-Saharan Africa, including economic assistance, food aid, the Peace Corps, and military assistance, have ranged from a peak of $2.2 billion in FY1985 to a low of $1.1 billion in FY1990 (both figures in constant 1996 dollars). Bilateral aid rose slightly after FY1990, but in recent years it has fallen off once again, as indicated in Table 2, which focuses on obligations, or actual commitments of aid funds to recipients. (Obligations differ from annual appropriations, since they may include funds appropriated in previous years and other funds that may become available.) In FY1997, bilateral aid obligations will approximate the 1990 low, as would the Administration's FY1998 request, if approved. (For details on the programs listed, see text, below.)

The aid peak in the mid-1980s reflected the high levels of foreign affairs spending characteristic of the period, which in turn grew out of the global competition with the Soviet Union. The special

[54]

Table 2. U.S. Bilateral Aid Obligations to Sub-Saharan Africa

(obligations, $millions)

	FY1994	FY1995	FY1996	FY1997 (est.)	FY1998 (request)
DFA	743.5*	690.8*	675.0	729.3	700.0
Ec. Support Fund	16.1	5.0	0.7	17.2	25.0
P.L. 480, Title I	26.9	24.6	0	0	0
P.L. 480, Title II	467.7	484.0	399.4	204.3	262.1
P.L. 480, Title III	86.3	53.0	25.0	28.4	19.9
Sec. 416 Food	14.8	1.1	0	0	0
Peace Corps	62.8	55.1	51.8	53.4	52.9
Military Aid Grants	0.5	0	5.0	7.7	10.0
IMET (military)	4.0	4.9	6.0	7.3	8.0
Total	1422.7	1318.5	1162.9+	1030.7	1078.0

*USAID's Africa Bureau provides DFA funds to the Global Bureau, and small amounts to other bureaus, for Africa projects. These funds are not included in the most recent data USAID provides for these years. Consequently, the amounts understate DA somewhat in comparison with figures for FY1997 and FY1998, which do include these funds. Earlier USAID data stated gave an FY1995 DFA figure of $822.3 million. The FY1996 figure anticipates that DFA obligations for the year will exceed the DFA appropriation when final data are available.
SOURCE: Data provided by USAID.

attention given to combatting famines afflicting several African countries at the time also boosted U.S. aid.

Global foreign assistance spending began to decline after the mid-1980s, and the Africa aid program fell in response. The decline was in part a reflection of mounting concerns over the size of the U.S. budget deficit and measures to bring the deficit under control. Toward the end of the decade, moreover, competition with the Soviet Union in the Third World began to fade as a U.S. priority. In addition, the United States cut aid to some countries that had been major aid recipients, such as Zaire and Liberia, because of human rights violations and political instability, or because the recipients refused to carry through with economic liberalization programs.

The reduction in Africa aid during the 1980s took place almost entirely within the security-oriented programs: military assistance and especially the Economic Support Fund (ESF). ESF aid is a type of economic assistance allocated by the State Department, in consultation with USAID, with the objective of promoting U.S. security interests. By the mid-1980s, many in Congress and in the wider aid-oriented community had come to believe that security assistance programs in Africa had grown too large and that more U.S. aid should be used to promote long-term development. This concern, combined with declining anxiety over the Soviet threat, brought a sharp reduction in the ESF.

Apart from ESF aid, a few African countries regarded as strategically important, such as Sudan, Kenya, and Somalia, once received substantial grants for the purchase of military equipment, but this sort of aid was also dropping as the 1980s ended. By FY1995, military grants or financing to purchase equipment had been phased out, and military aid was largely confined to small training grants, typically ranging between $100,000 and $200,000, funded under the International Military Education and Training (IMET) program. The State Department explains the continuing IMET programs in terms of promoting professionalism and respect for democracy and human rights—and of enhancing capabilities for participation in peacekeeping operations. The Administration's request for FY1998 does include $5 million in military aid grants to help Eritrea, Ethiopia, and Uganda strengthen their defense capabilities against the destabilizing threats posed by Sudan. A grant is also requested for the Administration's proposed new African Crisis Response Force (ACRF), which is to be composed of troops contributed by African armies.

Africa receives some security-related funds under the Peacekeeping Operations (PKO) account, authorized by Part II, Chapter 6 of the Foreign Assistance Act of 1961 (P.L. 87-195, as amended). Aid under this program has gone to assist peacekeeping by the West African states in Liberia and to strengthen the peacekeeping capabilities of the Organization of African Unity. This aid is not broken out in the Africa "all spigots" bilateral aid tables appearing in the USAID Congressional Presentations, but is included under PKO assistance reported in other tables. PKO aid has been used to increase the peacekeeping and conflict resolution capabilities of several countries. In FY1998, the Administration has requested $15 million for the ACRF.

Development Fund for Africa. Falling ESF levels threatened the overall scale of the sub-Saharan aid program after 1985, and this threat led to the creation of the Development Fund for Africa (DFA), which specifically earmarked a minimum level of DA for the region. The DFA guidelines first appeared in the conference report (H.Rept. 100-498) accompanying the FY1988 appropriations legislation and were enacted into law in 1990 (P.L. 101-513, Section 562), becoming Chapter 10 of Part I of the Foreign Assistance Act of 1961.

The DFA legislation authorizes assistance for a broad range of objectives. These reflect various development theories and strategies that had emerged in the development debate among policy-makers, academics, NGOs, the IFIs, and others over many years. According to Chapter 10, the purpose of the program "is to help the poor majority of men and women . . . to participate in a process of long-term development through economic growth that is equitable, participatory, environmentally sustainable, and self- reliant." Moreover, according to the law, DFA aid is to be used to "promote sustained economic growth, encourage private sector development, promote individual initiatives, and help to reduce the role of central governments

Figure 1. Bilateral Aid

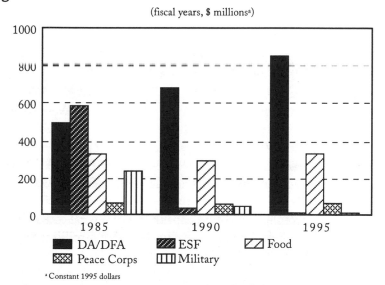

(fiscal years, $ millions[a])

DA/DFA ESF Food
Peace Corps Military

[a] Constant 1995 dollars

in areas more appropriate for the private sector." Chapter 10 stresses local involvement and "grassroots" development, but it permits
aid in support of economic policy reforms that promote several "critical sectoral priorities." These are agricultural production and natural resources, with an emphasis on promoting equity in rural
incomes; health, with emphasis on maternal and child health needs;
voluntary family planning services; education, with an emphasis on
improving primary education; and income-generating opportunities for the unemployed and underemployed. In addition, Chapter
10 authorizes aid for regional integration and donor coordination.

The DFA, with its broad phrasing and support for long-term funding, gave USAID planners new flexibility in designing the Africa-
assistance program. However, Congress did include guidelines
stating that a minimum of 10% of DFA funds should be devoted
to each of three broad purposes: agricultural production, health, and
voluntary family planning services. The overall effect of the decline
in ESF assistance and the creation of the DFA on the structure of
Africa's bilateral aid is illustrated in the figure (above), which com-
pares the aid program's structure in 1985, 1990, and 1995. The
DFA reached a peak of $800 million for FY1991 and remained
close to this level for some time despite efforts by some Members
to increase it to $1 billion or more. (See Table 3 for the leading DFA
recipients.)

Food Aid. Food aid to Africa fluctuates in response to the continent's needs. In FY1993, when a major drought afflicted eastern and
southern Africa, food aid amounted to 43% of bilateral aid, but in
FY1994, when conditions improved, it dropped to 27%. In FY1996,
bilateral food aid to sub-Saharan Africa totaled $425.5 million, or
about 35% of aid to the region. Most of Africa's food aid is in the
form of emergency grants given under Title II of the P.L. 480 program. This program is implemented by USAID in cooperation with
the Department of Agriculture. On rare occasions, countries in a
position to repay are given long-term, low-interest loans to purchase
food under Title I of P.L. 480. Some of Africa's poorest countries
have received U.S. food donations under Title III, entitled "Food
for Development," which can be used in feeding programs or sold

Table 3. Leading DFA Recipients

(obligations, $millions)

	FY1996[a]	FY1997 (est.)	FY1998 (request)
South Africa	122.4	89.7	70.0
Mozambique	51.3	31.0	39.2
Ethiopia	39.8	38.3	48.3
Uganda	39.6	41.4	49.5
Ghana	39.3	41.3	38.4
Malawi	33.8	36.1	37.4
Mali	30.3	32.0	36.0
Senegal	25.0	23.3	27.1
Kenya	24.3	20.2	20.0
Tanzania	23.3	18.7	20.0
Zimbabwe	23.3	18.1	15.3
Zambia	20.8	17.1	17.6
Madagascar	20.1	18.3	18.5
Benin	16.5	13.9	16.2
Angola	15.9	11.5	12.8
Guinea	15.2	13.8	14.0

[a] These figures reflect USAID estimates before Africa Bureau funds were allocated to the Global Bureau and other bureaus for Africa-related projects.

on the open market, with proceeds to be used for development purposes. Title III programs are underway in Ethiopia and Eritrea, and one is expected to begin shortly in Mozambique. A few countries have benefitted under Sec.416(b) of the Agricultural Act of 1949, as amended, which permits donations of surplus food to developing countries, emerging democracies, and relief organizations. (For further information, see CRS Issue Brief 95088, *Agricultural Export and Food Aid Programs*; and CRS Report 94-303, *P.L. 480 Food Aid: History and Legislation, Programs, and Policy Issues*.)

Africa's food situation appears to be fairly good at present, and food aid is not expected to be a major issue in 1997. Over the long term, some observers are concerned that food security in Africa will be undermined by rapid population growth, budgetary constraints in donor countries, and a decline in food surpluses as major food producers adopt more market-oriented policies. (For more information, see *International Relations: Food Security in Africa*. Testimony of Harold J. Johnson, Associate Director, General Accounting Office. GAO/T-NSIAD-96-217.)

Peace Corps. Funding for the Peace Corps, which currently has over 2,000 volunteers in 32 sub-Saharan countries, comprised about 4% of U.S. bilateral Africa aid in FY1996. Under the Peace Corps Act (P.L. 87-293), volunteers are to help the poorest people of these countries meet their basic needs, to promote a better understanding of the American people, and to promote a better understanding of other peoples on the part of Americans. In Africa, the Peace Corps attempts to accomplish these objectives through small-scale projects in agriculture, education, health, the environment, small business development, and urban development. Political instability and war have hampered Peace Corps efforts in recent years, forcing withdrawals from Rwanda and Burundi, Zaire, and the Central African Republic. At the same time, new programs have been launched in Ethiopia and Eritrea, where decades-long civil conflicts have ended, and the Peace Corps plans to begin operations in South Africa in 1997. The Peace Corps will leave Botswana in 1997 and Swaziland in 1998 to accommodate budgetary constraints and concentrate resources where they are most needed. The largest programs are in Mali, Ghana, Malawi, Cameroon, and Lesotho.

African Development Foundation. The African Development Foundation (ADF) has a unique mandate to make small grants directly to African cooperatives, youth groups, and other self-help organizations. These grants range from less than $20,000 to a maximum of $250,000. In addition, the ADF supports grassroots development research by African scholars and promotes the dissemination of development information at the community level. By law, the ADF is limited to 75 employees. Its 7-member Board of Directors must include 5 private-sector representatives. ADF does not station U.S. employees in overseas posts, but instead works through local-hires and periodic field visits.

The creation of the ADF in 1980 reflected a widespread view among many development experts—and in Congress—that foreign policy considerations were playing too large a role in the U.S. development aid program for Africa; that the USAID bureaucracy tended to delay the delivery of needed assistance; and that existing aid was governed by a "trickle down" philosophy that could be combatted by delivering some aid directly to poor Africans and their community organizations. Legislation establishing the ADF (P.L. 96-533, Title V) stated that its purposes were to strengthen the bonds of friendship between the people of Africa and the United States; support local self-help activities in Africa; stimulate participatory development; and promote the growth of indigenous development institutions (P.L. 96-533, Title V). The organization began operations in 1984, and a provision that would have terminated the ADF in 1990 was repealed in 1989.

Refugee and Disaster Assistance. The United States responds to African humanitarian crises in part with Title II food aid, discussed above, and in part through its refugee and disaster assistance programs. Most refugee assistance comes from the Migration and Refugee Assistance account of the State Department appropriation and goes to the United Nations High Commissioner for Refugees and international organizations, as well as private and voluntary organizations assisting African refugees. In FY1996, an estimated $175.4 million went to African refugees through this account, and the expenditure is expected to be about the same in FY1997. In addition, the Emergency Refugee and Migration Assistance (ERMA) account, created in 1962 to deal with unexpected refugee situations, has been drawn upon for African emergencies several times in recent years. ERMA funds were used in 1994, for example, to respond to the Rwanda refugee emergency. In September 1995, $20 million was authorized to meet the emergency needs of refugees from Rwanda and Burundi. (For further information, see CRS Issue Brief 89150, *Refugee Assistance in the Foreign Aid Bill: Problems and Prospects.*)

USAID's Office of Foreign Disaster Assistance (OFDA) also plays a major role in responding to African crises. In FY1995, it spent $116 million in dealing with 24 sub-Saharan disasters. The largest amount, $32 million, went to assist Angolans recovering from two years of renewed civil war, and large amounts were also spent in response to the humanitarian emergencies in Rwanda and Liberia.

Multilateral Assistance. The United States provides aid to Africa indirectly through international financial institutions (IFIs) and United Nations agencies. World Bank lending through its "soft loan" affiliate, the International Development Association (IDA) is the largest single source of development capital in Africa. IDA loans are considered a form of aid since they are virtually interest-free and carry extended repayment periods. The $2.7 million approved for Africa by IDA in 1996 includes $654 million to strengthen public sector management, $421 million for transportation, $328 million for agriculture, and $257 million for the "social sector," including $120 million for social rehabilitation in formerly war-torn Ethiopia. In addition, $408 million was approved for "multisector" loans to assist efforts by the recipient countries to carry out free market economic reforms. Loans in the other sectors were often linked to reform efforts as well. (World Bank, *Annual Report, 1996*).

Since the United States has contributed 17.7% of IDA's lendable resources, it could be argued that the United States was responsible for about $432 million of 1996 IDA loans to Africa. Economic analysts have technical reservations about tracing U.S. funds through IFIs to specific countries and regions, but it is clear that indirect U.S. aid to Africa through the World Bank was substantial. Some analysts are concerned that U.S. cuts in its contributions to IDA could lead other donors, many of which also face budgetary constraints, to follow suit, substantially diminishing IDA's lendable resources in future years. (For further information, see CRS Issue Brief 96008, *Multilateral Development Banks: Issues for the 105th Congress*, by Jonathan Sanford.)

In the past, the African Development Fund (AFDF) has been another major channel for indirect U.S. aid to Africa. The Fund is the soft loan affiliate of the African Development Bank (AFDB), which was initially established in 1964 as an all-African lender. Outsiders were invited to join the AFDF, created in 1973 to make concessional loans to the poorest African countries, and the United States became a member in 1975. The Bank itself, which holds 50% of the voting power in the AFDF, was opened to outside participation in 1983.

Congress appropriated $135 million as the U.S. contribution to the Fund in FY1994 and $124 million for FY1995. The executive branch used approximately half of the FY1995 appropriation to clear up arrears in U.S. contributions, but the remainder was held pending completion of negotiations on the seventh replenishment of the AFDF by donors. The House and Senate then voted to rescind the remaining $62 million of the FY1995 contribution, and no funds were approved for the Bank and the Fund in FY1996. The Bank and the Fund have installed new management, and the Administration requested some funding for FY1997, including a $50 million contribution to the Fund. Congress, however, made no appropriation for the Bank or the Fund.

Additional amounts of indirect aid reach Africa through U.S. contributions to the United Nations. These include contributions to the regular budgets of U.N. agencies active in Africa, such as the Food and Agriculture Organization (FAO) and the World Health Organizations, as well as voluntary contributions to various U.N. programs, particularly the large programs of the U.N. Development Program (UNDP) and the United Nations Children's Fund (UNICEF). The U.S. contribution to Africa through UNICEF in 1995 can be calculated at about $48 million, while the 1994 contribution through UNDP was about $20 million. (Calculated using data in UNICEF and UNDP annual reports. For further information, see CRS Issue Brief 86116, *U.N. System Funding: Congressional Issues.*)

Total U.S. Assistance. Total U.S. aid to Africa would be difficult to calculate exactly, partly because of the uncertainty attached to attributing a specific share of World Bank aid to the United States, and partly because of the difficulty of identifying every U.S. program that in some way benefits Africa. Adding the principal aid programs identified above, however, yields a total of about $2 bil-

Table 4. Estimate of U.S. Africa Aid
FY1996 ($millions)

Bilateral	1,162.9
PKO	9.0
ADF	11.5
Refugees	175.4
ERMA	0
OFDA	116.0 (FY95)
IDA	432.0
AFDF/B	0
UNICEF	48.0 (1995)
UNDP	20.0 (1994)
Total	1,974.8

lion (Table 4). Comparable calculations result in estimates of about $2.5 billion in 1994 and $2.3 billion in 1995. The totals would be somewhat larger if all of the smaller channels for U.S. funds, such as the full range of U.N. activities or U.S. Information Agency study grants, were factored in. The Assistant Secretary of State for Africa, speaking at a January 1995 press conference, included U.S. contributions to peacekeeping in Africa as aid and came up with a 1994 aid total of $3 billion.

Comparison with Other Regions. Some advocates of increased aid to sub-Saharan Africa contrast the Africa aid levels with aid to Egypt and Israel. Others see no issue in the disparity between Africa aid and aid to the Middle East or other regions, arguing that the differences reflect varying U.S. interests. Israel and Egypt together received $5.3 billion in bilateral assistance in FY1996—a level of aid that exceeds all forms of assistance for the 47 recipient countries in sub-Saharan Africa. On a per capita basis, about $2 was given in aid for each sub-Saharan African person, as against $100 per person in Israel and Egypt, or about $750 per capita for Israel alone. Bilateral aid for Africa is less than the $2.3 billion (FY1996) provided to the 35 recipient countries in Europe, including Russia; but bilateral Africa aid is greater than comparable assistance to Latin America and the Caribbean.

Comparison with Other Donors. In 1994, the United States was the second leading development assistant to Africa after France, which makes sub-Saharan Africa a special foreign policy focus. In 1995, however, according to data compiled by the Organization for Economic Cooperation and Development (OECD), the United States fell to fourth place, giving $1.024 billion in net bilateral Official Development Assistance (ODA), which includes food aid and relief, while France gave $2.378 billion, Japan $1.25 billion, and Germany $1.097. Some 14 developed countries gave a larger proportion of their net ODA to sub-Saharan Africa in 1995 than did the United States. Ireland, for example, gave 86% of its ODA to the region, while France gave 49%, the United Kingdom 50%, and Germany 35%. The figure for the United States was 32%. (OECD, *Development Cooperation*, Development Assistance Committee 1996 Report.)

Recent Trends in U.S. Aid. The Clinton Administration has set its own "strategic objectives" for development aid, and USAID's FY1995 congressional presentation identified four of these—building democracy, stabilizing population growth, protecting the environment, and achieving broad-based economic growth—as most appropriate for Africa. In the FY1998 presentation, the growth objective—rephrased as "broad-based economic growth with equity" was listed first, while "fostering democracy and participation" was listed as the fourth objective. A fifth objective is to provide "emergency relief to help nations make the transitions from crisis to longlasting development." USAID's annual presentations relate DFA expenditures in each country to these strategic objectives rather than to specific provisions of the DFA legislation.

The emphasis on democracy in the DFA precedes the Clinton Administration. USAID began to develop programs for democracy support and to introduce democratic criteria for sub-Saharan recipients in 1990, during the Bush Administration, anticipating democracy support efforts in Eastern Europe and the former Soviet Union. The shift toward building democracy is reflected in the changing identities of the leading U.S. aid recipients. In 1985, Sudan, Somalia, Liberia, Kenya, and Zaire topped the list of recipients, and none of these had a democratic government. By 1995, South Africa, where a democratic election took place in 1994, was the top recipient by a wide margin, while the other leading recipients were all undergoing democratic transitions.

USAID officials have testified that the United States has had a number of successes in its efforts to promote democracy through the foreign assistance program. They point to Ghana, Uganda, Zambia, Mali, and South Africa as countries where sustained USAID projects and programs helped move the democratization process forward. Critics of USAID's democracy programs, noting, for example, widespread reports of corruption and undemocratic practices in Zambia, question whether democratic reforms in several recipient countries are genuine or will endure. USAID officials respond by acknowledging that problems inevitably arise in democratization and insisting that long-term development programs can't be interrupted every time this occurs. While assistance will be cut off when there are persistent problems, as has happened with Togo, or directed solely through NGOs, as in Nigeria, USAID maintains that aid should continue to countries that aren't yet fully democratic but are moving in the right direction.

A USAID report, *Africa: Growth Renewed, Hope Rekindled*, claims broad successes for DFA projects in promoting both economic and political democracy during the period 1988–1992. USAID also maintains that the DFA has assisted in helping African countries achieve increases in child immunization and the use of oral rehydration therapy, shift their health policies towards an active emphasis on AIDS prevention, increase the prevalence of contraceptive use, and boost primary school enrollments. In agriculture, USAID asserts that the DFA has helped liberalize agricultural markets, increase smallholder production; and facilitate the development of new seed varieties. The DFA has also been used to assist governments undertaking macro-economic reforms, including reductions in the size of government bureaucracies and the privatization of government enterprises. USAID maintains that it has introduced an efficient, performance-based management system for the DFA, and focused

U.S. resources on countries where the chances for success are greatest. USAID is closing its missions in several sub-Saharan countries in keeping with the downsizing affecting the foreign affairs agencies generally. Most are in countries that are not cooperating with USAID's efforts to promote democratic and free-market reforms, while the Botswana closing reflects the country's "graduation," as its annual per capita income approaches $3,000. Some believe that the shutdowns will boost USAID's efficiency over the long-term, but others worry that a major retrenchment is beginning. In their view, U.S. influence will suffer as a result.

Stabilizing population growth has been an important objective of the Clinton Administration's Africa program—and one that is often emphasized by Administrator Atwood. Policy planners believe that the continent has little prospect for economic growth, ending famine, or reducing conflict unless population growth can be slowed. USAID officials believe that reductions can be achieved because, they argue, family planning is winning wider acceptance among African themselves and because some African governments have come to accept the need for smaller families. USAID points to declining fertility rates in Kenya, Zimbabwe, and Botswana as evidence of these trends and notes that the United States is the largest donor of population assistance in each of these countries. USAID population efforts focus on persuading senior African policy planners of the need to stabilize population growth; supporting family planning programs; supporting population planning education and information programs; and developing channels for the distribution of contraceptives. (USAID Congressional Presentation, Fiscal Year 1995).

The Clinton Administration has launched several special development initiatives in Africa. The Greater Horn of Africa Initiative (GHAI), aims at easing the perennial food insecurity in a region extending from Eritrea and Ethiopia to Tanzania by promoting collaboration and consultation on food security strategies. The Initiative for Southern Africa, which will total $300 million over five years, reflect's USAID's recognition of the region's economic potential and its desire to reinforce South Africa's democratic transition as a model for the rest of the continent. The initiative includes a Democracy Fund, to make grants in the region in support of democracy, and a Southern Africa Enterprise Development Fund (SAEDF), to promote indigenous business development and ownership. USAID is proposing to devote $20 million annually to the SAEDF over 5 years.

The Leland Initiative is a 5-year $15 million program aimed at connecting 20 sub-Saharan countries to the Internet. The initiative is named for the late Representative Mickey Leland, founder of the House Select Committee on Hunger, who died in a 1989 plane crash while on his way to investigate conditions in an Ethiopian refugee camp. Technicians from several U.S. Government agencies are working to implement the project, which will make Internet access available to "all sectors of the African development community," including NGOs, government agencies, "private developers," and individuals. (USAID press release, June 6, 1996.)

In testimony before the House Africa Subcommittee on March 13, 1997, USAID's Acting Assistant Administrator for Africa, Carol Peasley, described a 10-year Food Security Initiative, to be launched with a $30 million pilot project in FY1998. Peasley said that trade and investment in Africa would be receiving increased emphasis through programs to help African countries create "the appropriate enabling environment."

South Africa has been a special focus of the Clinton Administration's aid policy in Africa. After the installation of a democratically-elected government in May 1994, President Clinton pledged the United States to $600 million in aid to South Africa over three years. An estimated $544 million of this amount is expected to come from USAID programs, with an emphasis on three sector areas: black private sector development, jobs, and infrastructure; strengthening democratic and political institutions; and education and health delivery. In addition, the United States is guaranteeing loans for housing, electrification, and small business development. Resources are also being used to support the growth of small, medium, and micro-enterprises (SMMEs) in South Africa. USAID Administrator Atwood announced in February 1996 that the agency would "begin a process of phasing down" the South Africa program, because South Africa was acquiring the resources to deal with its own development problems.

Background Materials

Current Policy Debate

In Africa, and among many academic experts, a debate continues to rage over conditions on aid imposed by western donors, including the United States, requiring free-market reforms and progress toward democracy. Many critics of "conditionality" acknowledge that such reforms may have value over the long term but insist that they are not sufficient to spark an era of economic growth. Instead, they maintain, Africa needs help with building basic infrastructure, creating an industrial base, and improving education before substantial growth can occur. In the short term, some maintain, free market reforms can be detrimental to Africa's efforts to build an economic base, since African producers are not yet ready to face international competition. Democratic reforms may be threatened, some argue, by political tensions resulting from the stresses of economic change. Democratic reforms can themselves prove detrimental, in the view of some critics, if they are introduced in a way that intensifies ethnic conflict.

The French government has shown some sympathy to African views on conditionality, and President Chirac has said that African countries should be permitted to find their own way to a democratic future, at their own pace. In Washington, however, the wisdom of conditionality is now widely accepted, and policy seems unlikely to change. From the U.S. perspective, private investment, particularly foreign investment, and expanded international trade are vital to accelerating African economic growth—and these require free markets. Democratization, meanwhile, is seen as essential to creating stable and responsive governments—and to reducing corruption.

U.S. Interests in Africa. Proposals that would reduce aid to Africa reflect an underlying view that aid should be directly related to U.S. interests—and that the United States has few such interests in Africa. During the Cold War, proponents of this view concede, there may well have been a global-strategic rationale for spending in Africa, but today, they argue, neither economic interests nor strategic concerns are sufficient to justify maintaining a substantial Africa assistance program. They accept that in Eastern Europe and the former Soviet Union, the United States has a clear interest in promoting a permanent shift to democracy and free market systems. But they see few such interests in Africa, and little prospect that aid would be effective in promoting them. Nor do they see significant prospects for U.S. business in sub-Saharan Africa, since exports to Africa are about .9% of total U.S. exports, while imports are 1.7% of the U.S. total (1995 data).

Supporters of maintaining or increasing aid levels for Africa argue that it is a mistake to focus solely on immediate economic and strategic concerns in evaluating U.S. interests. Many maintain that the United States has a special responsibility in sub-Saharan Africa, growing out of historic and cultural links to the region, that exceeds any political or economic interest. They note that U.S. relief organizations, churches, and African-American groups have shown a strong humanitarian interest in promoting development and combatting suffering in Africa. Moreover, some insist that there are broader, long-term interests in Africa that should not be ignored. In their view, the United States can help to create an international system congenial to its interests by supporting development, transitions to democracy, and free market economies everywhere, not just in Eastern Europe and the former Soviet Union. Many see concrete economic gains from African development. On February 3, 1995, USAID Administrator Atwood spoke forcefully of sub-Saharan Africa as an emerging market, nearly at the stage today's "Asian tigers" were in 1960. Supporters of U.S. aid to Africa often cite the potential for trade and investment in southern Africa; the mineral wealth of South Africa and several other countries; and the oil reserves along the West African coast. They note that total U.S. trade with sub-Saharan Africa, at $18 billion in 1995, exceeds trade with Eastern Europe ($13 billion, 1995), including Russia.

Consequences of an Aid Reduction. Proponents of reducing aid for Africa do not anticipate significant negative consequences, partly because they do not believe there are substantial U.S. interests in Africa, and partly because they doubt that past aid has had much real effect. Africa's many negative economic indicators, including widespread declines in per capita incomes and food production, have led many to ask what has been accomplished by the foreign assistance given to Africa in the 30 to 35 years since most countries became independent. Skeptics point out that major former recipients of U.S. aid, including Sudan, Liberia, Somalia, and Zaire, have fallen into eras of collapse from which they have yet to recover. Most skeptics of aid to Africa accept that disaster relief should be provided when these humanitarian disasters occur, but they believe that funds for promoting development, democracy, or economic reform are likely to be wasted.

Supporters of the Africa aid program, by contrast, insist that aid reductions would have serious negative consequences. Atwood and others argue that Africa suffers from a bad press and that genuine progress toward democracy and economic reform has been made in a number of recipient countries, including Ghana, Malawi, Mozambique, Namibia, and South Africa. Treasury Secretary Robert Rubin pointed out on April 21, 1997 that "market reforms have also taken hold, and in response the region's annual growth rate has risen from 1.4% over the period of 1991 to 1994, to 4% in 1995. Some countries . . . have growth rates in the 5 to 7% range, while a very few, like Uganda, grew by 10%." Others note progress in health, family planning, the environment, and famine prevention. (Gary Gaile and Alan Ferguson, "Success in African Social Development: Some Positive Indications." *Third World Quarterly*, September 1996.) Aid reductions could undercut USAID support for programs that combat the spread of HIV infection, some note, even though AIDS could have disastrous consequences for South Africa and other countries if not slowed. It is less costly to try to prevent disasters by promoting development and democracy today, according to aid backers, than to mount huge relief operations when African societies break down.

Ending the DFA Earmark. Those who favored eliminating the earmarks for the DFA insist such a step need not eliminate development aid to Africa—only that the Africa aid program should not be regarded as a "perpetual entitlement." (Remarks by Senator McConnell at a Dec. 12, 1994, press conference.) With the DFA earmark eliminated, from this point of view, Africa aid could be flexibly adjusted by policymakers in relation to changing U.S. interests.

This sort of flexibility has not been provided policymakers to date because language supporting a proportionality formula in the appropriations legislation has tended to protect Africa's share of the overall development aid program. Nonetheless, supporters of Africa aid worry that the earmark's elimination represents a significant break with established practice and could undermine the continent's aid levels in the future. While they welcome the proportionality formula, they see it as the result of compromises that might not be achievable in future years.

Aid versus Trade in an Era of Reduced Funding. Representatives Philip Crane, James McDermott, Charles Rangel and several other Members have formed the bipartisan African Trade and Investment Caucus to reexamine U.S. aid policy priorities. As the name of the Caucus suggests, members believe that more emphasis should be placed on promoting trade with Africa and U.S. investment in Africa in order to spark economic growth—particularly since funding for traditional development assistance programs will likely continue to be constrained. Those who have reservations about the Caucus approach acknowledge that promoting trade and investment could benefit Africa and the United States, but they oppose diverting development assistance funds for this purpose. In their view, the United States should maintain, or if possible expand, its development programs and projects, both on humanitarian grounds and to help Africa create the economic base needed to meet stiff global competition for markets and investment funds.

On April 24, 1997, Representative Crane and others introduced a bill, the African Growth and Opportunity Act (H.R. 1432), aimed at increasing Africa trade and investment while including a number of provisions intended to respond to the concerns of potential critics (see below, Legislation). On February 18, the Clinton Administration had released its own report to Congress highlighting Africa's trade potential. (See CRS Report 97-494 F, *Africa: Trade and Development Initiatives by the Clinton Administration and Congress.*)

H.R. 1757

Foreign Relations Authorization Act. Sec. 2301 permits development aid to Congo notwithstanding Sec. 620(q) of the Foreign Assistance Act of 1961 or any other provision of law. Amendment by Rep. Donald Payne agreed to by voice vote, June 10, 1997. Bill passed the House June 11. Senate version lacks a comparable provision. Passed the Senate, amended, June 17, 1997.

H.R. 1759 (Gilman)

Foreign Assistance Reform Act. Authorizes $700 million for the DFA in FY1998 and the same amount in FY1999; authorizes $11.5 million for the ADF in FY1998 and $10 million in FY1999; in addition, authorizes $2.5 million in FY1998 DA funds and $4 million in FY1999 funds for the ADF; authorizes $600 million for each of the two fiscal years for a worldwide Child Survival and Disease Programs Fund; authorizes $32 million in each fiscal year for debt relief for poor countries worldwide; authorizes debt-for-equity swaps, debt-for-development swaps, or debt-for-nature swaps; calls for the study of the appropriateness, feasibility, and costs of establishing a Radio Free Africa. Introduced and referred to the Committee on International Relations, June 3, 1997. (This bill consisted of the foreign assistance portions of an earlier bill, H.R. 1486, which had been marked up and reported. See CRS Report 97-533 F, *Foreign Relations Authorization Act (H.R. 1757): House Consideration.*)

H.R. 1432 (Crane)/S.778 (Lugar)

African Growth and Opportunity Act. As introduced, requires the President to convene annual meetings of U.S. and African officials to foster close economic ties; creates a United States-Sub-Saharan Trade and Economic Cooperation Forum; declares that a U.S.-Sub-Saharan Africa Free Trade Area should be established; requires the President to develop a plan for entering into trade agreements with African countries, abolishes textile import quotas for Kenya and Mauritius, subject to certain conditions; states sense of Congress that debt owed to the United States should be extinguished for the poorest African countries that are heavily indebted and pursuing growth-oriented policies, and that the Overseas Private Investment Corporation should establish equity funds to support projects in sub-Saharan Africa; requires President to appoint a United States Trade Representative for Africa. Introduced on April 24, 1997, referred to the Committee on International Relations and to the Committees on Ways and Means and Banking and Financial Services. International Relations Subcommittee on Africa consideration and markup, May 22; committee consideration and markup June 25; ordered to be reported.

S. 955 (McConnell)

Foreign Operations Appropriations. Does not earmark the DFA; states that up to $10.5 million may be made available for the ADF; prohibits foreign military financing for Sudan and Liberia; prohibits direct aid to Sudan; prohibits aid to Liberia, Sudan, and Congo (formerly Zaire), except through regular notification procedures of the Committee on Appropriations; includes no funding for the AFDF; provides $2.9 million for the Communal Areas Management Programme for Indigenous Resources (CAMP-FIRE) in Zimbabwe; permits funding for Liberia notwithstanding prohibitions on aid to countries in default on U.S. debt; report raises concerns over 90,000 individuals detained in Rwanda and denies funding to the Administration's proposed African Crisis Response Force. Reported by the Committee on Appropriations (S.Rept. 105-35) on June 24, passed the Senate on July 17, 1997.

NICOLAS VAN DE WALLE AND TIMOTHY A. JOHNSTON

"IMPROVING AID TO AFRICA"

Overseas Development Council Policy Essay, October 1996*

Foreign aid to sub-Saharan Africa can claim many individual successes over the past 30 years. Yet despite unprecedentedly high levels of aid in recent years, the continent's development performance has been disappointing. Aid alone cannot ensure development and should not be blamed whenever development fails to occur. Nonetheless, the need to make aid more effective is widely recognized. Africa's need for aid remains high, given the continent's prevailing levels of poverty and inability to attract private foreign capital. If, as now seems likely, the level of aid is going to stagnate or even decline in coming years, the impact of aid activities has to be increased to allow Africa to escape from its current economic crisis and meet its development challenges. Political support for aid to Africa has declined in the developed countries at least in part because of the widespread perception that aid to the region has been ineffective. This "aid fatigue" is often based on misperceptions and overgeneralizations, but in the long term, aid will clearly have to become more effective.

Aid has been the subject of much research in the policy and scholarly communities. Although much analysis and many recommendations have been lavished on improving the giving of aid by donors, surprisingly little attention has been devoted to improving

---

*This excerpt is reprinted from Nicolas van de Walle and Timothy A. Johnston, *Improving Aid to Africa*, Policy Essay No. 21 (Washington, DC: Overseas Development Council, 1996), pp. 1–9. For the full text of this essay or a copy of this excerpt in French, please contact the Overseas Development Council, 1875 Connecticut Avenue, NW, Suite 1012, Washington, DC 20009.

the use of aid by African governments themselves. The Project on Aid Effectiveness in Africa, a collaborative research effort involving paired research institutes in seven donor and African countries, was initiated to help address this oversight and to examine ways to improve the aid relationship. It constitutes the most ambitious policy analysis ever undertaken of how African governments manage aid. It has involved detailed case studies in seven African nations (Botswana, Burkina Faso, Ghana, Kenya, Senegal, Tanzania, and Zambia), conducted by African universities and research institutes in collaboration with policy institutes from seven donor countries (United States, France, United Kingdom, Japan, Canada, Denmark, and Sweden, respectively). This essay synthesizes the project and offers recommendations for improving aid effectiveness.

THE IMPACT OF AID TO AFRICA

The essay assesses the impact of aid on development as well as its record of promoting institution building. Aid to Africa has contributed to many important achievements over the past several decades. Individual aid efforts have helped to improve physical infrastructure, improve health and education, and introduce new agricultural technologies across the African landscape. Roads and bridges have been constructed, schools and universities built, central banks established, and hundreds of thousands of Africans sent abroad for scientific and technical training.

At the same time, aid has not succeeded in fostering economic growth and poverty alleviation in most African countries. From 1980 to 1993, the continent's rate of economic growth was actually negative. Although aid helped to improve indicators of human welfare such as literacy and infant mortality rates, Africa continues to lag behind other regions of the developing world.

It is difficult to untangle aid from other factors that may have influenced the region's economic growth and development, including the recipient government's macroeconomic and sectoral policies, the nation's endowment of physical and human resources, prevailing political systems, and the international environment. A host of factors have clearly mitigated the impact of aid. Many of aid's achievements in the 1960s and 1970s were negated by the counter-productive policies of governments in the region. These policies, as well as a sharp decline in international commodity prices, pro-duced a debilitating economic crisis and placed governments under added pressures. Political instability and civil conflict reversed the achievements made in some countries. In sum, despite significant achievements, aid has not led to sustained economic growth in most African countries.

No challenge is more pressing or more difficult than that of devel-oping institutional capacity in Africa. Significant progress has been made in the education and training of individual Africans, but aid has had a disappointing record of promoting institution building. Although many if not most of Africa's public institutions were created and have been sustained with the help of substantial donor support, these institutions are weak and highly dependent on out-side resources.

KEY WEAKNESSES IN AID TO AFRICA

Four critical deficiencies help to explain the disappointing perfor-mance of aid to Africa. In each case, problems were either caused or exacerbated by weaknesses in the government's own management capabilities.

Lack of Recipient Ownership
The importance of recipient "ownership" of development projects and programs is widely acknowledged. Recipient governments and beneficiaries can be said to "own" an aid activity when they believe it empowers them and serves their interests. Low ownership of aid is common across Africa. Donors tend to dominate the aid process and to pay inadequate attention to the government's own prefer-ences. For their part, cash-strapped governments, with weak tech-nical capacity, tend to defer to donor expertise and rarely identify their own priorities for aid in an explicit fashion.

Poor Coordination of Aid

The number of donor agencies and aid projects has increased spectacularly. Most African countries receive aid from more than a hundred bilateral, multilateral, and nongovernmental organization (NGO) agencies, each with its own procedures, priorities, planning cycles, and reporting requirements. Recipient governments must exhaust their limited managerial capacities to track these projects and integrate them into their own development strategies. In addition, the proliferation of projects and donors increases the risks of duplication and waste. Thus, the need to coordinate donor efforts is well recognized. The donors have established various mechanisms to facilitate coordination, but the results have been disappointing. In truth, aid coordination is most effective when it is undertaken by recipient governments, which are best placed to integrate the efforts of numerous donors into a national development strategy. Too often, African governments have not played this role.

Inability to Cover Recurrent Costs

The inability of governments to cover recurrent costs and counterpart obligations undermines the impact of aid in many African countries. Too often, the achievements of aid-funded projects are not sustained when donor funds end. Governments sometimes simply lack the funds to honor their recurrent costs and obligations. In addition, African governments and donors continue to plan inadequately for counterpart and recurrent expenditures. Some countries, like Botswana, have effective mechanisms to control and monitor the costs associated with donor projects, which are integrated into the government's overall development management. In most countries, aid activities are not fully integrated into national budgeting and planning exercises. For their part, donors often fail to recognize the problem and fail to plan for the withdrawal of aid.

The Proliferation of Stand-Alone Projects

Aid too rarely contributes to effective institution building because local institutions are bypassed in the design and implementation of projects. The donor preference for enclave projects and parallel management structures is particularly destructive. Rather than integrate their aid within government ministries, donors often resort to mechanisms and structures that demarcate their own activities. This ensures greater flexibility in the short run and may help projects attain short-term goals, but it complicates sustainability, undermines ownership, and makes overall government coordination of the aid effort virtually impossible.

In sum, the failure to integrate aid into the government's own development management efforts is typically a root cause of many of the common problems that undermine the effectiveness of aid. Governments often lack the commitment or capacity to play an active role in the design, implementation, and evaluation of aid, instead allowing donors to make key decisions regarding how aid moneys will be spent. For their part, donors often adopt practices that make it hard for governments to integrate aid into their own planning and budgeting. Both tendencies undermine the impact of aid.

REASONS FOR DONOR PERFORMANCE

Aid agencies recognize many of the problems identified in the case studies. Yet reforming donor practices that undermine capacity building in recipient countries has been slow and uneven, largely because of two factors. First, objectives not related to the needs and capacities of the recipient countries have often motivated the giving of aid. In particular, too often the motivations have been foreign policy and commercial objectives rather than the economic development of Africa. During the Cold War, the need to maintain allies in the region or to ensure stability dictated much aid. Today, commercial motives continue to lead donors to adopt practices, such as aid tying (linking foreign aid to the purchase of goods and services from firms in the donor country), which are inefficient and tax the management capacities of governments.

Second, the motivations, constraints, and deficiencies of the aid bureaucracies themselves undermine the development of government capacity. For instance, the proliferation of individual, stand-alone projects is due largely to the need to placate domestic critics of aid and to the incentives facing donor agency staffs. Similarly donors are uncomfortable with the loss of discretionary control that government coordination of aid implies for their own programs. As a result, change is unlikely to occur unless recipient governments impose it.

REASONS FOR RECIPIENT PERFORMANCE

Recipient governments do not address the common problems undermining aid for several reasons.

First, the nature of governance in Africa has shaped the ability and commitment of governments to promote effective aid. At independence, the top priority of most African governments was to secure political stability. This need motivated many of the practices that have reduced the effectiveness of aid, including the rapid growth of the civil service through systematic patronage, the expansion of the economic role of the state, notably with the establishment of a large number of parastatal organizations, and the implementation of policies that undermine economic growth.

Second, the economic policy environment has lowered the quality of public-sector management and, through it, the effectiveness of aid in most African states. The case studies confirm that the policy environment is likely to affect the effectiveness of aid resources. Economic policies that lead to balance-of-payments difficulties, high budget deficits, or high rates of inflation are likely to produce a climate of economic uncertainty and stagnation, which puts additional stress on the administration and further weakens the quality of its management.

Macroeconomic instability has engendered a vicious cycle: the onset of instability typically spells the end of long-term development planning, as governments seek short-term expedients to address their immediate problems. Pressures on the fiscal balance have led governments to reduce the rate of public investment in favor of preserving public consumption at current levels, largely for political reasons. Almost invariably, the capital budget takes the brunt of the first budget cuts, while politically sensitive civil service salaries and public services are protected; as the crisis persists, the government increasingly skimps on maintenance and operating expenditures.

Third, when it persists over several years, economic crisis has an increasingly pernicious effect on public institutions. Fiscal crisis leads governments to cut back on recurrent expenditures, ultimately threatening their capacity to undertake even routine tasks. Many of the most skilled civil servants begin to depart for more lucrative careers in the private sector or abroad. In many countries, the day-to-day operations of public institutions are seriously compromised by missing parts, equipment breakdowns, unpaid bills, absent personnel, and the suspension of services.

THE REFORM OF AID

Aid is capable of promoting economic growth in Africa. For it to do so, however, the capacity of African states to manage aid resources has to improve. This entails making sure that aid is better integrated into the government's overall development planning and budgeting. The needs of the population and the capacity of recipient governments to use aid resources effectively should determine the flow of resources that each country receives.

RESTORING MACROECONOMIC STABILITY

The ability of African governments to manage aid resources more effectively should be enhanced so that aid can promote growth and poverty alleviation. Economic stabilization is a critical prerequisite for effectiveness. As long as African countries remain in fiscal disequilibria, their governments will not be able to undertake long-term planning and institution building. Aid resources can and should be used to help governments stabilize their economies, but only if the government is fully committed to stabilization.

LESSENING THE BURDEN OF AID

A number of measures should be undertaken to lessen the managerial burden of aid on governments.

First, recipient governments should coordinate aid resources, rather than allow donors to dominate the process. To facilitate this, donors should specialize in specific sectors, reduce the number of projects, and streamline and simplify their programs and procedures.

Second, program aid, though often less taxing on government capacities than project aid, is typically more fungible, which means that it is less likely to alter the spending patterns of the government. Therefore, it is not likely to promote development in the absence of sound economic policies. In such situations, donors should maintain a policy dialogue with the government but limit aid flows and direct them to project assistance, often focusing on nonstate actors. When sound economic policies have been put in place, donors should expand program aid, perhaps in the context of sectoral investment strategies negotiated with the government.

Third, the increasing reliance on NGOs to design and implement aid projects may not be compatible with effective aid because public intervention is often needed, for example, to support recurrent costs. In such instances, donors should not rely on NGOs. Where public intervention is not needed, perhaps because of the use of cost-recovery mechanisms or the presence of local community support, the devolution of aid to NGOs is sound practice and should be encouraged.

IMPROVING THE RECIPIENT MANAGEMENT OF AID

Donors and governments can undertake a number of measures to increase the capacity of governments to manage aid resources effectively.

The first condition for improving government management of aid is to reform and strengthen the civil service, which has been decimated by the effects of economic crisis and the neglect of donors and governments. A strong civil service is an obvious prerequisite

[82]

for more effective government, but thorough civil service reform is bound to take considerable time. In the meantime, strengthening and empowering senior officials in the planning units of central ministries would allow governments to begin to assess needs systematically, establish priorities, and plan the use of aid resources. In addition, the deterioration of Africa's national statistical services and other sources of information critical for policymaking needs to be reversed.

Second, the relationship between donor and recipient must be changed. In particular, governments must play a more proactive role in the design, implementation, and evaluation of projects and in the overall coordination of aid programs. Certainly, for the current incentives to change, donors should reward governments that integrate aid into coherent development strategies, and they should directly help governments to enhance their capacity in this sphere. Variants of the so-called Foundation Model need to be tested, in which responsibility for identifying needs, designing projects, and evaluating the results rests with the government, while donors engage in continuous policy dialogue, provide technical assistance as needed, and evaluate the government's aid performance without intervening on a day-to-day basis in aid activities.

Third, greater accountability and transparency are needed to improve the performance of public administrations in Africa. Donors should support the current wave of political liberalization and democratization across the continent because it heralds the emergence of civic associations, a freer and more active media, and the empowerment of local communities, all of which counterbalance the power of the central state. Democratization will have a slow and uneven impact on African life, but it has the long-term potential to make governments more responsive to the needs of their citizens.

Finally, broader public discussion regarding the management, evaluation, and hidden costs of aid is needed to make governments accountable for their use of aid resources. The local press and various professional and civic associations should be encouraged to sponsor and engage in public debates about aid and its priorities, strengths, and weaknesses and the potential changes from which it might benefit.

JONATHAN E. SANFORD

"AFRICA'S DEBT BURDEN: PROPOSALS FOR FURTHER FORGIVENESS"

CSIS Africa Notes, October 1996*

At their October 1996 joint annual meeting, the World Bank and the International Monetary Fund (IMF) will consider a new proposal for reducing the foreign debt burden of the world's poorest countries. Sub-Saharan Africa would be the principal beneficiary.

THE AFRICAN SITUATION

Most analysts agree that sub-Saharan Africa is seriously burdened by foreign debt. (Unless otherwise noted, all figures on sub-Saharan Africa appearing in this paper exclude South Africa and Namibia, in order to give a more accurate picture of the situation facing Africa's nonindustrial countries. "Africa" is sometimes used as shorthand for the sub-Saharan region.) The problem is not the absolute size of the debt ($199 billion). Other regions owe much more. Rather, the burden arises from the size of the debt relative to the area's struggling economies. As Table 1 indicates, the region's 1995 debt equaled 119 percent of its combined gross national product (GNP) —three to four times the ratio for most other developing areas. Similarly, sub-Saharan Africa's debt was almost four times as large as

*CSIS Africa Notes is a briefing series designed to serve the special needs of decision-makers and analysts with Africa-related institutions, universities, and other arenas. It is a publication of the African Studies Program of the Center for Strategic and International Studies, Washington, DC. CSIS is a private, nonpartisan, nonprofit policy research institute founded in 1962.

[84]

Table 1. Income and Debt Burden of Developing Areas (1995)

	Foreign Debt	Debt-per Capita	Debt-GNP Ratio	Debt Export Ratio	Debt Service Ratio	GNP per Capita	Avg. Growth (1980-93)
Region	($billion)	(%)	(%)	(%)	(%)	($)	(%)
Sub-Saharan Africaª	199	384	119	389	20	362	-0.8
Latin America	607	1,302	40	254	30	1,003	-0.1
East Asia/Pacific	373	276	29	83	11	951	6.4
South Asia	168	140	39	246	25	362	3.0
Eastern Europe/ Central Asian	380	768	36	145	15	2,127	-0.3
Middle East/ North Africa	217	827	40	137	14	2,054	-2.4

ª Excluding South Africa and Namibia (except for annual growth rate figure).
SOURCES: World Development Report 1995 (World Bank); Africa data supplied by World
  Bank.

its export income. Although Africa spends a lower proportion of
its export income on debt service than does Latin America or
South Asia, the Latin region has a higher per capita income, and
South Asia's record of sustained economic growth has eased its debt-
repayment burden. Africa, by contrast, has experienced grinding
poverty and persistent economic decline. The subcontinent is
simply too poor to service its debt and meet its basic economic requirements at the same time.

Table 2. Sub-Saharan Africa's Long-Term and IMF Debt (1994)

Creditors	Share of Debt (%)	Share of Repayments (%)	Net Transfer on Debt ($billion)
Bilateral	46	23	-0.55
MDBs	31	41	1.53
Private	19	28	-1.50
IMF	4	7	0.32
(Amount in $billion)	(162.5)	(8.2)	(-0.20)

SOURCE: World Bank

Unlike some developing regions, sub-Saharan Africa owes most of its long-term foreign debt (81 percent) to official bilateral or multilateral creditors rather than to private lenders (see Table 2). This means that creditor country governments will have to play a leading role in any alleviation of African debt.

The multilateral development banks (MDBs) and the IMF are currently the only categories of foreign creditors whose new lending to Africa exceeds repayments to them in connection with old loans (i.e., they are making a positive net transfer of resources to the region). In 1994, the MDBs disbursed $4.901 billion in new money to the sub-Saharan region while they received $3.369 billion in debt-service payments. The World Bank accounted for most of the MDB total. Nearly all its loans to Africa were made on concessional terms. The IMF disbursed $918 million for new "purchases" while it received $598 million for "repurchases" and charges. Most of the IMF's new credits to the region are via its concessional loan "window," the Enhanced Structural Adjustment Facility (ESAF).

Bilateral creditors disbursed $1.34 billion in new money to the sub-Saharan region in 1994, while receiving $1.893 billion in principal and interest payments. Bilateral loans are not the whole picture, however. According to the World Bank, outside governments made grants totaling $11.5 billion in 1994 and $13 billion in 1995 to aid sub-Saharan Africa. As described below, they also forgave several billion dollars in bilateral debt owed by African and other low-income countries.

Private creditors disbursed $804 million in new money to the subcontinent in 1994, while taking out $2.31 billion in debt service. They also forgave about $2.68 billion owed them by African countries between 1991 and 1995 and extinguished $189 million through debt swap agreements, thereby eliminating some 7.8 percent of the total that had been owed to them in 1990.

ACCESS TO IMPORTS

Sub-Saharan Africa's ability to import would probably be enhanced by a reduction of its debt-service burden. Those countries currently servicing their debts could free up some of the money hitherto spent for that purpose to purchase imports needed for development. For those countries not servicing their debts, a debt reduction might remove a factor discouraging investment by private investors and lenders.

Such outcomes are not automatic, however. Countries would need to discipline themselves so that, after debt forgiveness, money now earmarked for debt service would not be dissipated on consumption or military equipment. Likewise, African countries wanting to attract investors would still need to adopt policies fostering economic growth as well as political reforms promoting stability, accountability, and effective government.

BILATERAL DEBT FORGIVENESS

For several years, creditors have realized that many severely indebted low-income countries cannot repay all they owe. The Group of Seven (G-7) countries—United States, Germany, Japan, France, Britain, Italy, and Canada—have taken the lead in devising plans to deal with this situation. Those plans have been put into effect by the Paris Club, an informal forum where debtor countries can reschedule or restructure the debts they owe bilaterally to foreign governments.

In 1988, following a G-7 meeting in Toronto, the Paris Club approved a menu of options, known as Toronto Terms, whereby creditor countries could forgive up to one-third of the net present value of eligible debt owed them by low-income countries. Normally, the Paris Club reschedules debt payments only currently in arrears or due in the next 18 to 24 months. Previously rescheduled debt and payments for debt contracted after a cutoff date (usually one prior to the country's decision to seek Paris Club help) are generally not eligible for rescheduling. Between 1988 and 1991, the Paris Club rescheduled on Toronto Terms $5.4 billion owed by 19 African countries and $0.3 billion owed by one other country.

In 1991, following a G-7 meeting in London, the Paris Club agreed to expand its debt forgiveness menu. Called Enhanced Toronto Terms (or, more recently, London Terms), the new arrangement provides for forgiveness of up to half the debt eligible for rescheduling owed by low-income countries. Between 1991 and 1995, under Enhanced Toronto Terms, the Paris Club rescheduled about $5.5 billion owed by 20 African countries and $3.6 billion owed by three other countries.

In December 1994, following an earlier G-7 meeting in Naples, the Paris Club agreed that, instead of simply writing off some arrears and upcoming payments, creditors could eventually forgive as much as two-thirds of the total debt owed them by eligible countries. In 1995, the Paris Club rescheduled on Naples Terms $987 million owed by eight African nations and $476 million owed by four other countries. Another $110 million of Uganda's debt was rescheduled immediately.

Until 1993, the United States chose not to forgive any debt through the Paris Club. In 1989 and 1991, however, Congress adopted legislation authorizing the President to forgive debt owed by low-income countries. Under these rules, the United States forgave $2.65 billion owed by low-income countries (including $1.08 billion owed by sub-Saharan African nations). Many of these countries had all or most of their debt forgiven.

In 1992, according to U.S. Treasury figures, the 28 countries that seemed eligible for Paris Club debt forgiveness owed the United States $4 billion. Almost three-quarters ($2.8 billion) was owed by four countries (Liberia, Somalia, Sudan, and Zaire) that lacked governments or had governments that few wished to reward through debt forgiveness. Bilateral debt owed to the United States amounted to only a small fraction of the $71 billion the 28 countries owed their bilateral creditors or the $104 billion they owed all official creditors.

In 1993, the Clinton administration announced and Congress approved plans for U.S. participation in Paris Club debt forgiveness agreements. In 1993 and 1994, the U.S. government forgave through the Paris Club another $1.7 million each owed by Niger and Senegal.

Background Materials

THE TRADITIONAL MULTILATERAL STANCE

Opposition to Forgiveness/Rescheduling

Thus far, the international financial institutions have rejected any notion of writing off debt owed them by borrower countries. The IMF says that its key role in the world monetary system precludes such concessions. The MDBs, meanwhile, have argued that debt forgiveness might force them to pay more for their loans and that they would have to pass this increased cost on to their borrowers. This would amount to asking middle-income countries to pay the price of forgiving debt owed by low-income borrowers.

Expanded MDB Lending

Instead of forgiving debt, the MDBs have lent more to low-income areas. Disbursements to sub-Saharan Africa from the World Bank's concessional loan "window," the International Development Association (IDA), grew from $424 million in 1980 and $1.69 billion in 1988 to $2.89 billion in calendar 1994. An additional $928 million was disbursed to these countries in 1994 by the African Development Fund (the concessional loan "window" of the African Development Bank) and other multilateral institutions (mostly Arab-financed).

IDA loans are available only to the world's poorest countries. They are repayable over a period of up to 50 years without interest but with a three-fourths of 1 percent annual service charge. The amount owed by African countries to IDA grew tenfold between 1980 and 1994, from $2.58 billion to $25.16 billion. Their annual debt-service payments to IDA grew correspondingly from $22 million in 1980 to $251 million in 1994. The annual net transfer on debt from IDA to sub-Saharan Africa has grown from $403 million in 1980 to $2.64 billion in 1994.

Meanwhile, because the World Bank is making few loans to these countries through its market-rate loan "window," the International Bank for Reconstruction and Development (IBRD), their outstanding debt to the IBRD has declined from a peak of $9.18 billion in 1990 to $8.07 billion in 1994. IBRD disbursements fell to $392 million in 1994; African repayments to the IBRD exceeded this amount by $1.37 billion. The other MDBs received $152 million more from Africa in 1994 for debt service on market-rate loans than they disbursed in new loans.

Other Steps
In 1989, the World Bank created a Debt Reduction Facility for IDA-Only Countries, to help low-income countries retire at deep discounts some of their debt to commercial banks. It transferred $100 million to the Facility that year, using some of the IBRD's net income, and transferred another $100 million to the Facility in 1994 from the same source. Using these funds and money contributed by donor countries, the Debt Reduction Facility made grants through August 1996 totaling $361 million to 12 low-income countries. With this help, the recipients were able to buy back and extinguish (at an average 13 cents per dollar) $2.82 billion in principal owed to commercial banks. Eight sub-Saharan African countries expunged $1.11 billion in debt.

The World Bank has also sought to help some of its low-income borrowers handle their outstanding IBRD debt. In 1988, it created the Fifth Dimension program, which assists heavily indebted poor countries that were previously creditworthy enough to borrow from the IBRD but are now eligible to borrow only from IDA. Under the program, they can borrow extra money, as part of new IDA adjustment loans, to cover the current interest cost of their old IBRD loans. In effect, the program turns IBRD debt into IDA debt for a year, at least as far as interest costs are concerned. Between 1989 and 1994, these loans financed roughly 25 percent of the IBRD debt service due from participating countries. Of the 17 recipients of Fifth Dimension loans, 11 were African countries.

THE NEW WORLD BANK/IMF PROPOSAL

Since 1994, the United Kingdom and subsequently other major industrial countries have been pushing the multilateral institutions publicly to do something about the multilateral debt problem.

Consequently, in 1995 and 1996, the World Bank and the IMF started drawing up a plan.

On September 14, 1995, the *Financial Times* (London) reported on a draft World Bank internal study of the debt issue. In July 1995 a Bank task force had proposed that the Bank and the IMF create a new multilateral debt facility (MDF) to help poor countries retire some of their debt to the multilateral institutions. The World Bank staff estimated that $11 billion—obtained from IBRD net income and contributions by bilateral donors—would be needed over several years. The IMF, Japan, and other major countries reportedly opposed the proposal, although U.S. officials said they were "cautiously positive."

On March 6, 1996, the World Bank and IMF staffs sent a revised plan entitled *A Proposed Initiative for Assisting Heavily Indebted Poor Countries* to their executive directors. The principal goal remained reduction of overall poor-country debt to sustainable levels. Now, however, a multistage process was envisaged in which most of the debt reduction would be carried out through increased forgiveness by bilateral and commercial creditors. Debt owed to the multilateral institutions would be reduced only after the other creditors had written off most of the debt the poor countries owed to them.

The World Bank and IMF executive boards endorsed the debt plan in early 1996. Subsequently, the joint World Bank/IMF Development Committee—a high-level panel composed of finance ministers from key World Bank and IMF member countries—approved the plan's basic principles at its April 23, 1996, meeting in Washington, D.C., but called for refinement of certain details. The Development Committee asked the World Bank and IMF staffs to consult broadly and prepare an action program for consideration at the next IMF/World Bank annual meeting.

At a late June 1996 economic summit meeting in Lyons, France, the leaders of the G-7 countries announced their support for the World Bank/IMF debt plan, endorsed a proposal that the IMF sell some of its gold ("resources held by the IMF") to finance increased ESAF lending, and concurred that bilateral creditors should go "beyond the Naples terms" in forgiving bilateral debt owed by poor countries.

World Bank President James Wolfensohn announced, at the G-7 meeting, that he would ask the Bank's governing board to transfer $500 million from IBRD net income to help finance multilateral debt relief. The G-7 welcomed his proposal and suggested that the World Bank allocate $2 billion for this purpose in future years. They said that the regional MDBs should take similar steps to alleviate the debt burden of their poorest borrowers.

Sustainability and Eligibility

Under the World Bank/IMF plan, each participating borrower would have enough debt forgiven to reduce its debt burden to sustainable levels. The plan defines "sustainability" as a situation in which the ratio of the present value of a country's foreign debt to its export income is in the 200 to 250 percent range and the country's debt-service ratio (the ratio of debt-service payments to export income) is between 20 and 25 percent. Criteria for eligibility include a per capita income below the IDA operational threshold ($865 per year) and an economy that is not creditworthy. The latter criterion excludes "blend" countries (which borrow some of their World Bank funds from the IBRD) such as India, China, Nigeria, and Zimbabwe. The World Bank and IMF staffs estimate that 8 to 12 countries have "unsustainable" debt burdens, as defined by the plan, and that another dozen are "possibly stressed" and might need debt relief under the plan.

Amount and Pace of Forgiveness

In the first stage of the World Bank/IMF plan, the Paris Club would continue rescheduling poor-country debt on Naples Terms. Creditors would then conduct a case-by-case examination of each debtor's situation. If the Paris Club's application of Naples Terms had brought a country's debt ratios down to sustainable levels, no further forgiveness by the multilateral institutions would be contemplated. However, if a country's debt-service or debt-export ratios were still too high, or if special problems made its situation precarious even at "sustainable" levels, the World Bank/IMF plan provides for a new round of debt forgiveness.

In this second stage, all bilateral creditors would be asked to reduce the net present value of the debt owed them by the debtor country by 90 percent of its original level. Commercial creditors would also be asked to write off 90 percent of the debt owed them. In some instances, this could be accomplished by broadening the list of debt eligible for adjustment through the Paris Club process.

At the end of three years, if 90 percent of the bilateral and commercial debt had been written off and if the country had successfully implemented the required reforms (see below), the World Bank and the IMF would take another look at the country's debt situation. Only at this point, if the debt burden were still too heavy, would the World Bank expunge enough debt to make the burden sustainable.

The IMF plays a crucial role in the multilateral debt plan. To receive Paris Club debt forgiveness, countries must have in place a stabilization or adjustment program approved by the IMF. Most heavily indebted low-income countries cannot afford the rate (4.3 percent annually, as of July 1996, repayable three years from the date the funds are drawn) the IMF charges for its regular standby loans. Consequently, the IMF provides most of its assistance to these countries via the ESAF, its concessional loan facility. ESAF loans are repayable over ten years at an interest charge of one-half of 1 percent. Under the World Bank/IMF plan, the ESAF's resources would be expanded substantially and the repayment period for ESAF loans would be doubled to 20 years.

The IMF estimates that by 2005, as the flow of repayments increases from the Structural Adjustment Facility (the ESAF's predecessor), the ESAF will be largely self-financing. The ESAF's existing resources will be largely exhausted, however, by 1999. Between that year and 2005, the ESAF will have insufficient funds to meet the increased pace of new IMF financing that the World Bank/IMF debt plan will require. Under the plan, the IMF will be expected to provide a major share of the funding needed to close the anticipated gap in ESAF resources.

Conditionality

To qualify for second-stage debt relief under the plan, debtor countries would need to undertake a three-year program of economic adjustment and reform in "partnership" with the World Bank or the IMF. The goals and performance criteria for the three-year program would probably be comparable to those of regular adjustment (standby or ESAF) programs.

Who Pays?

No debt owed to the MDBs or the IMF would be formally forgiven. Instead, the World Bank would channel contributions from IBRD net income and bilateral donors into a special fund that would be used to pay off some of the debt owed to the MDBs. The IMF would also reduce the net present value of its claims on a country by making it new ESAF loans. Thus, the poor countries' debt burden would be reduced in a manner that allowed the international financial institutions to preserve their record of never rescheduling or forgiving debt.

IMF Managing Director Michel Camdessus proposed in early 1996 that the IMF use 10 percent of its gold reserves to help close the anticipated gap in ESAF resources. The IMF lists most of this gold on its books at the original value of SDR 35 (about $50.78 as of mid-1996) an ounce. Camdessus said that some IMF gold could be sold (the market rate being about $395 an ounce in mid-1996), with the proceeds going to the ESAF to fund additional concessional lending to low-income countries.

The IMF articles of agreement require an 85 percent vote by the membership before the IMF can sell gold. Several countries (notably Germany, France, and Switzerland) have expressed strong reservations. Some have suggested that the IMF should instead borrow money, using part of its gold as collateral. That money could be used directly (or it could be invested and the profits lent instead) to facilitate debt relief for poor countries. Camdessus has reportedly decided, meanwhile, that fewer countries than he originally thought are likely to contribute to the ESAF. Consequently, he has reportedly proposed that the IMF sell or pledge more gold (perhaps 15 percent of the total) to help finance the anticipated increase in ESAF lending.

The World Bank and IMF staffs say that the debt plan will require an additional $7 billion to $8 billion in debt forgiveness (in present value terms) over and above the forgiveness already available from the Paris Club on Naples Terms. If bilateral and commercial creditors write off 90 percent of the debt owed to them, multilateral debt relief will (the IMF and World Bank staffs estimate) account for about one-third of the above total.

ALTERNATIVES TO THE WORLD BANK/IMF PLAN

Many analysts consider the official World Bank/IMF debt relief plan incomplete and inadequate. A number of alternative plans have been circulated that call for greater levels of multilateral debt relief. Four examples follow.

Option 1: A Multilateral Facility to Cover Payments
One option would have the multilateral institutions manage a fund to cover the poor countries' multilateral debt payments for an extended period. To qualify, debtor countries would need to undertake major reforms in their economic policies, procedures, and institutions.

One proponent of such a solution is Matthew Martin (a British international financial analyst). In a recent report prepared for the "Group of 24" developing countries, he endorses the World Bank staff's July 1995 proposal that the Bank and the IMF create a multilateral debt facility, but argues that the $11 billion price tag cited at the time was unnecessarily alarming. Because the MDF would not cancel debt up front, the full $11 billion would not be needed right away. Rather, Martin says, the money would be spent over the course of 15 years (at a rate somewhere between $467 million and $734 million annually) to help poor countries make their scheduled multilateral debt payments as long as they continue pursuing acceptably sound economic policies.

It is important, Martin emphasizes, that the resources used to fund multilateral debt relief be "additional"—not the same resources the MDBs and the IMF would otherwise use to fund new loans to poor countries. A considerable amount of aid is currently being lost, he claims, to "subtractionality." Bilateral aid is diverted from development purposes to help poor countries meet their multilateral debt-service obligations. Many MDB loans are defensive in nature, designed mainly to help countries meet their multilateral payments. Multilateral debt forgiveness would mean that new bilateral and multilateral aid could go for development programs rather than for merely paying the cost of old aid loans.

Option 2: A Multilateral Facility to Clear Debt
A second option would have the multilateral institutions create a multilateral debt facility for the purpose of reducing the size of the poor countries' multilateral debt. Arguably, this would cut debt-service payments and lay the groundwork for new inflows of foreign private credit and investment. Percy Mistry, a British international financial analyst and former World Bank staffer, is a proponent of this view. He characterizes the World Bank/IMF plan as seemingly having been designed more to protect the multilateral institutions than to help the poor countries. He wants his proposed MDF to be independent of the MDBs and the IMF, to keep them from using it to protect themselves at the expense of other creditors.

Option 3: Forgive More MDB Debt Promptly
The third option would cut the poor countries' debt to multilateral institutions promptly and substantially, targeting the benefits of debt relief primarily to the poor. One adherent of this view is the charitable organization Oxfam International, which argues that the World Bank/IMF plan underestimates the number of countries likely to qualify for assistance and the cost of providing relief.

While agreeing that debt relief should be conditioned on debtor willingness to adopt needed policy reforms, Oxfam does not accept that the IMF should take the lead in monitoring compliance or that the IMF's standard prescription for stabilization or adjustment should be the benchmark for measuring cooperation. Instead, Oxfam argues that the conditions for debt relief should be based on targets that reflect local conditions and are consistent with the goal of reducing poverty. In particular, the multilateral institutions should require debtors to use any funds freed up by debt forgiveness for new investments aimed at meeting basic human needs.

Option 4: Forgive All Debt Owed by Poor Countries
Some observers want multilateral creditors to forgive much or all poor-country debt. Proponents of this view include the Fifty Years Is Enough Campaign and the British-based Jubilee 2000 Campaign, as well as many church bodies.

The Fifty Years Is Enough Campaign calls on the World Bank to write off everything owed to the IBRD by severely indebted low-income countries (per capita GNPs below $675) and half of the IBRD debt owed by severely indebted middle-income countries (per capita GNPs between $676 and $2,695). The Campaign also wants the IMF to forgive all low-income country debt and half of all middle-income debt. If this were done, the World Bank would forgive about $7 billion owed by low-income countries and about $17 billion owed by middle-income countries. The IMF would write off $6.7 billion owed it by low-income countries and $13.4 billion owed it by middle-income debtors. For sub-Saharan Africa alone, the World Bank would write off about $7.9 billion and the IMF $6.3 billion in debt.

The Jubilee 2000 Campaign calls for the extinguishing of all debt owed by 35 African countries to private or official creditors—a step that would expunge (using World Bank figures for 1994) some $74 billion owed to bilateral creditors, $50 billion owed to MDBs, $7 billion owed to the IMF, and $31 billion owed to commercial creditors (see Table 2).

Many proponents of maximum debt relief want all multilateral debt forgiveness to be unconditional, often arguing that the economic policies associated with adjustment or stabilization plans hurt the poor and inhibit real development. In addition, they see debt reduction as only a first step. The Jubilee 2000 Campaign, for example, says that increased flows of assistance from the creditor countries will be needed for many years to produce long-term improvements in the borrower countries' situation.

CAN DEBT RELIEF SUCCEED?

Amount and Pace of Forgiveness
Sub-Saharan Africa's debt problem is probably more a symptom than a cause of the region's prolonged economic malaise. Nevertheless, most analysts agree that the debt burden is a major impediment to economic development and some type of debt forgiveness is required.

Should most of the debt owed by poor countries be expunged or should it simply be reduced to "sustainable" levels? In many respects, as Christopher Barrett, an economics professor at Utah State University, notes in a paper prepared for the 1996 International Studies Association conference, the "central point of confusion in the debate about African debt forgiveness is the amount of growth stimulus one can reasonably expect." Some analysts argue that a substantial and rapid reduction of the poor countries' stock of debt is a prerequisite for sustained economic growth. Others say that more real growth will result if the forgiveness process is gradual and focused primarily on reducing the poor countries' annual debt-service obligations.

Each side quotes econometric studies supporting or rejecting the proposition that the ratio of debt to income (the "debt overhang") is high enough in the case of the heavily indebted poor countries to harm economic development by discouraging investment and economic policy reform. The sides also disagree on the economic impact of other factors besides debt (e.g., corruption, political instability, and regional conflict) and on the possible impact of debt forgiveness on such concerns.

In addition, there is controversy over which option would better promote debtor-country adoption of new economic policies and procedures. Some argue that the debtors will adopt major economic reforms voluntarily once they are freed from the burden of excessive debt. Others believe that once a debt is forgiven, the creditor loses its leverage on the debtor country; therefore debtors will be more likely to adopt and follow through on reforms (which may be painful and costly in the short run) if creditors make their willingness to continue the process of expunging debt over time conditional on continued reform. The latter approach would probably be more acceptable to creditor-country governments, in part because gradual debt forgiveness would cost them less.

Both strategies seek to reduce debt-service payments, encourage economic reform, and attract private investment in the low-income countries. Large amounts of concessional debt would have to be forgiven up front to produce a modest decline in a country's annual debt payments. The same effect could be achieved by guaranteeing coverage for the poor countries' debt payments as they come due and requiring good performance as a condition for continued eligibility. Thus, the proponents of rapid and substantial debt reduction have not yet made the case that their approach would be more effective than a gradual one.

Most analysts see continued infusions of bilateral and multilateral aid and private loans and investments as important to the development of the poor countries once their debt burden has been relieved, but foreign aid donors and private-sector entities might be less inclined to put money there after having written off large debts by these countries. Low-income countries could find themselves worse off if debt relief means that new aid flows decline along with their indebtedness.

In the United States, for example, Congress must appropriate a sum equal to the actual present value of a bilateral loan before the loan can be forgiven. This appropriation will probably be charged against the budget of the agency on whose books the loan is carried. If large amounts of debt are written off, agencies may have little money available to fund other activities.

As of December 1994, countries in sub-Saharan Africa (not all of them eligible for Paris Club forgiveness) owed $5.951 billion to the United States for long-term foreign aid or export finance loans. If the net present value of this debt were, say, half its face value, Congress would have needed to appropriate about $3 billion to cancel the loans. In fiscal 1994, the U.S. government committed $3.25 billion for development, food aid, and emergency relief programs around the world. Thus, a 1994 decision to forgive all long-term African debt would have left almost nothing to fund U.S. aid anywhere in the world. (It should be noted that, in most cases, the annual debt payments made by African countries to Washington are only a small fraction of what they receive in new grant aid.)

The multilateral banks too have limits on their ability to absorb losses. Debt written off by their market-based loan programs (IBRD, etc.) would have to be charged against the banks' reserves or other assets. The multilateral development banks finance their market-based loans with borrowed funds. Even if they appraised the loans they forgave at less than face value, the MDBs would still have to pay their creditors the full face value of the debt they had incurred to fund those loans.

If the MDBs use an excessively large share of their financial assets to fund debt relief, their creditors will probably demand higher interest rates on the bonds the MDBs sell to fund their operations. This in turn would force the MDBs to charge higher rates of interest to middle-income borrowers. The middle-income countries would probably oppose any plan that might lead to such an outcome. Likewise, the advanced industrial countries, which own a majority of the World Bank's voting stock, are unlikely to support any plan that substantially increases their financial risk and IBRD liability.

In short, a debt plan aimed at immediate reduction of debt overhang may be too expensive to be workable. In contrast, a plan that focuses on reducing the burden of debt service would not require large up-front expenditures. A creditor could simply agree to waive collection of debt payments as they come due. Spreading the process out over time would make debt reduction affordable. Moreover, private entities might be more willing to risk money in a country if they knew that its future debt payments would be "sustainable" for a significant period than if they knew only that its debt burden was "sustainable" at one particular time.

Sustainability and Eligibility

The question of what constitutes a "sustainable" level of debt (the criterion that largely determines whether a country is considered eligible for multilateral debt relief) is marked by some controversy, but the differences between the World Bank/IMF position and those of most critics do not appear significant. Everyone seems to agree that whatever threshold is eventually adopted should not be applied mechanistically and that other factors should also be taken into account in determining relief eligibility.

The World Bank and the IMF seem to believe that they should be the final judges of whether a country's debt burden is "sustainable," while others argue that debtor countries should have a say in the determination, on the grounds that they know their situation best. Concern has also been expressed that the multilateral institutions might be tempted to protect their own interests at the expense of the debtors if they had sole power of judgment. The fact that the World Bank and the IMF claimed that only 12 countries were clearly eligible and another 12 were possibly eligible for relief under their debt plan might give some credence to this argument. The data in the World Bank's 1995 *World Debt Tables* show that many other countries not on the Bank/IMF list had debt ratios well in excess of the Bank/IMF's stated threshold for "sustainability." Evidently, countries are considered ineligible if they are already undertaking reforms. Some of the countries that do seem eligible will likely be disqualified because of their reluctance to reform.

It remains unclear whether bilateral aid should be counted in the calculation of a country's debt "sustainability." The World Bank/IMF plan appears to assume that present levels of bilateral aid will continue and that the aid can be used to offset debt-service obligations. Critics argue that bilateral grant aid is likely to decline in future years owing to budgetary pressures in donor countries and that in any case these funds are not always available to help countries service debt because they are often earmarked for particular development projects. Neither argument seems fully convincing; uncertainties and counterarguments abound. How this question is resolved will have a strong impact on the ultimate feasibility of the World Bank/IMF plan and on the number of countries that will qualify for debt relief under the plan.

Who Pays?

The World Bank and the IMF assume that they will need to spend about $2.3 billion to $2.6 billion to reduce the poor countries' debt to sustainable levels. The Fifty Years Is Enough Campaign argues that they should spend $13.7 billion to forgive debt owed by low-income countries and another $30.4 billion to help heavily indebted middle-income countries. Other analysts quote price tags ranging from $7–$11 billion (payable over 15 years) to $15–$18 billion (payable now).

The multilateral institutions could use several resources to help offset the cost of a debt-reduction program. Prominent among these are their financial reserves. Many analysts say these should be depleted, in whole or in part, to fund multilateral debt relief for poor countries.

The Fifty Years Is Enough Campaign calls on the World Bank to deplete its IBRD reserves to cancel debt owed by low- and middle-income countries. This proposal may be based on a misperception of the role of the Bank's reserves. The IBRD would probably not go out of business if it depleted its reserves in this manner, but it almost certainly would have to raise its interest charges and substantially restrict its operations. This would considerably reduce its effectiveness as a development and lending institution.

Other analysts suggest that the IBRD could spend $2–4 billion from its reserves to fund debt relief for poor countries without injuring its financial stability. This may be feasible. The IBRD's retained earnings (the largest component of its reserves) totaled about $15.5 billion in 1995; the ratio of retained-income reserves to outstanding loans was 10.4 percent. Reducing IBRD reserves by $2.5 billion, as Matthew Martin proposes, would lower the reserve-to-loan ratio to 8.4 percent. Reducing IBRD reserves by $4 billion, as Percy Mistry and Oxfam suggest, would lower the ratio to 7.2 percent. Such a ratio might be enough to cover present contingencies, but it might not be sufficient for the future. The Bank evidently plans to continue transferring a major portion of its net income each year to IDA, debt relief, and/or other special programs. If its reserves are not increased, the IBRD's reserve-to-loan ratio will decline as its outstanding loan balance increases, shrinking to perhaps 4 percent by 2000.

The Fifty Years Is Enough Campaign calls on the IMF to use its "$35 billion" reserves to cancel debt owed it by low- and middle-income countries. This proposal seems to be based on a misperception. The IMF does not have $35 billion in reserves. Its total subscribed quota in 1995 was worth about $227.8 billion. This money belongs to the member countries. When the IMF makes a loan, it borrows from the account of one country (paying interest) to obtain the funds it needs to execute that loan. If the IMF were to cancel repayment of debt owed to it, it would be unable to repay its own debt to its member countries. The IMF would have to add the cost of servicing that debt permanently to its operating budget or ask the United States and other creditors to forgive repayment of the IMF's debt. The IMF's reserves, about $2.8 billion in 1995, would be insufficient to cover the cost of funding debt forgiveness.

As of June 1995, the IBRD had a $3.74 billion loan loss reserve (separate from its main reserves). It was owed $4.47 billion by the 24 countries (18 African, 6 other) that seem eligible for assistance via the Fifth Dimension program. The use of about $1 billion to $1.5 billion from the loan loss reserve to write off some of the debt owed by these countries to the IBRD might be a reasonable step and perhaps a pragmatic acknowledgment that countries too uncreditworthy to qualify for new IBRD loans may also be too poor and uncreditworthy to repay their old IBRD loans.

How MDB bondholders would react to such an action is uncertain. They might regard debt reduction for poor countries as a way of strengthening the IBRD portfolio. On the other hand, bondholders might be upset (and demand higher interest in the future) if they see this as a first step toward eventual broader reduction of debt owed by middle-income countries.

An equally serious concern is the MDBs' future relationship with the former debtors. Should they make new loans, as though nothing had happened, or (consistent with their policy on overdue loan payments) should they stop all new lending? The answer may determine whether using the loan loss reserve to write off debt is a good idea from the perspective of borrower countries.

The IMF owns 103.44 million ounces of gold, worth about $40.88 billion. Most member countries now seem to agree that the organization should sell or pledge a limited share of this stockpile to finance debt relief through increased ESAF lending. This step could generate $3.6 billion to $5.3 billion for use in funding multilateral debt relief (once the IMF is reimbursed for the modest book value it accords its gold holdings).

The World Bank evidently plans to fund its participation in the Bank/IMF debt reduction plan with money from its annual net income. As noted earlier, Bank President Wolfensohn announced in June 1996 that he would ask the World Bank governing board to transfer $500 million for this purpose. (In 1995, the IBRD transferred from its net income $300 million to IDA and $20 million for emergency assistance to Rwanda. In 1994, it transferred $465 million to IDA, $100 million to the Debt Reduction Facility for IDA-Only Countries, and $50 million for aid to Gaza.) This annual amount could pay for major debt-overhang reductions in no more than a few countries, but it would be enough to let the Bank cancel a sizable share of poor-country debt payments as they became due during the next decade.

Critics argue that any funds used to forgive debt must be new money, not money that the MDBs would have otherwise used to help low-income countries. This seems a reasonable point. If one assumes that the IBRD will continue to transfer $300 million or more annually from its income to IDA, then an annual contribution for debt reduction (such as that proposed by Wolfensohn and the G-7 countries) would come from money that would otherwise go to IBRD reserves, not from funds otherwise destined to help low-income countries.

Except for the African Development Bank and the European Bank for Reconstruction and Development, the multilateral banks keep their books in U.S. dollars but use a variety of currencies in their operations. As the relative values of these currencies fluctuate, the values of MDB assets change accordingly. The banks record this change in their translation adjustment accounts. For the most part, any gains or losses are only hypothetical, because the MDBs do not trade currencies to realize in cash increases in the paper values of their currency translation accounts.

In 1995, the value of the World Bank's translation account increased by $1.9 billion to a cumulative total of $3.3 billion. The currency translation account for the Asian Development Bank increased by $72 million in 1995, to $307 million. On the other hand, the Inter-American Development Bank's account declined by $28 million in 1995, to $144 million. The changes were reportedly due mainly to a decline in the value of the U.S. dollar (down 1.8 percent in 1995 relative to the SDR).

Some observers have proposed that the MDBs use the money in their currency translation accounts to fund debt forgiveness for poor countries. If the banks do this, they will in effect be betting that the U.S. dollar will never increase in value again. Few currency experts would make this bet. If the dollar were to increase in value at some point after all or part of the translation accounts had been cashed in and used for debt relief, MDB assets would decline in value (in dollar terms). The resulting losses would have to be charged against paid-in capital or retained earnings. Thus, using temporary surpluses in the translation accounts to finance permanent debt reductions would be imprudent.

The World Bank/IMF plan (as well as some of the alternative proposals) assumes that donor countries will contribute several billion dollars to support debt reduction. Any such bilateral contributions may be smaller than anticipated, however. For example, it is noteworthy that U.S. Secretary of the Treasury Robert Rubin said in April 1996 that meeting the cost of reducing multilateral debt "should be done with the resources, or at least predominantly with the resources, of the IMF and the World Bank. We do not think [it] should require contributions from the donor nations." In June 1996, the leaders of the G-7 countries announced, at their summit meeting in Lyons, that they would support more bilateral debt forgiveness—if it were done "in conjunction with a maximum possible contribution by the World Bank and IMF."

Many Paris Club creditors believe that the World Bank and the IMF—which seem reluctant to forgive debt themselves—have not acknowledged the major effort these creditors have already made to provide debt relief. Many of these creditors want to see first what the World Bank and the IMF are willing to do before they commit themselves to any formal arrangement.

There seems to be no provision in the World Bank/IMF plan

for securing the participation of non–Paris Club creditors. For some debtors, the amounts owed to these creditors (Russia in particular) are substantial.

What about the plan's request that private creditors forgive 90 percent of the debt owed them by poor countries? If bilateral and multilateral creditors forgive a major share of the debt owed to them, the debt owed to private creditors is more likely to be paid. Thus, private creditors might be tempted to refrain from joining in a campaign of debt forgiveness.

Through August 1996, the World Bank's Debt Reduction Facility for IDA-Only Countries helped poor countries write off $2.82 billion owed to private creditors, at a cost to the Facility of $361 million, half of which came from the IBRD and half from bilateral donors. As of 1994, African countries owed private creditors $31 billion. Therefore a major new infusion of funds would be required if the Bank were to seek expansion of the Facility with an eye to helping extinguish 90 percent of this debt. It seems unlikely that bilateral donors would agree to cover half the cost, given the substantial burden they would have already assumed.

In effect, the World Bank/IMF plan makes the multilateral institutions the forgivers of last resort. The MDBs recognize that bilateral and commercial creditors may not agree to write off 90 percent of the debt owed to them. "It should be stressed," the World Bank and the IMF observe at the end of their official explanation of the plan, "that this share [a presumed one-third share for the multilaterals in the total cost of the plan] would be significantly higher if this assumption [90 percent forgiveness by other creditors] is not realized."

Conditionality

Some analysts want the multilateral institutions to forgive poor-country debt unconditionally. They assume either that removal of the debt will be sufficient to rectify the borrowers' problems or that the poor countries will take the right steps once they are freed from debt. Other observers, however, doubt the truth of both assumptions. In any case, the multilateral institutions and their major member countries will almost certainly require debtor countries to adopt new economic policies and procedures as a condition of debt relief.

What should those conditions be? Critics condemn the adjustment policies traditionally sponsored by the World Bank and the IMF on the grounds that austerity and budget cuts hurt the poor. The international financial institutions (IFIs) and their supporters, on the other hand, argue that countries experiencing chronic inflation and balance-of-payments deficits must inevitably undergo some form of adjustment. Having a program in place to shape and guide the adjustment process is better, they say, than allowing it to occur in a piecemeal and haphazard fashion.

Kinder, Gentler Adjustment?

The IFIs have sought to include "safety nets" in their recent adjustment programs to protect poor and vulnerable people. Critics argue that these "safety nets" do not always work and are at best only a mild antidote for the severe stresses that adjustment imposes on a borrower country. The IFIs and their supporters retort that the critics have proposed few alternative plans that will help poor countries improve their economic situations over a reasonable length of time without long-term foreign subsidies and without austerity or other negative economic effects.

Nevertheless, the multilateral institutions and their major member countries may find it difficult to build support for the World Bank/IMF debt plan if their critics (in debtor countries and in nongovernmental organizations) are concerned that a key element of that plan (increased ESAF lending by the IMF) could do more harm than good. A number of steps can be taken to ease this anxiety.

When ESAF assistance is being contemplated, the World Bank and the IMF collaborate on the preparation of a Policy Framework Paper (PFP) for the borrower country. Technically, the PFP is a statement by the borrower about its future plans and priorities. In practical terms, the IFIs have a major role in the PFP's preparation because of their leverage and because the borrower country often lacks sufficient capacity to prepare the paper itself. The IFIs could promote broader public understanding and soften resistance on the part of critics by making the PFP preparation process more transparent and by increasing the public availability of information about the terms and goals of ESAF adjustment programs.

Adjustment programs seek to change economic conditions in borrower countries. Unless resources, contacts, and skills are available, however, the borrower may not be able to take advantage of the improved environment. Thus, any country getting an ESAF adjustment loan should also get a parallel adjustment loan from IDA to facilitate the reforms and investments needed to expand production and promote the transfer of resources to more efficient uses. IDA might also make project loans in the borrower country to address needs and opportunities anticipated by the ESAF and IDA adjustment plans.

The debt-plan proposal to double the repayment period for ESAF loans to countries receiving debt forgiveness would diminish the repayment burden associated with these loans. The longer repayment period would also give the IMF a chance to lengthen the period within which the borrower is required to complete the adjustment process funded by the loan. Such an easing would make implementation less painful.

A final step addressing concerns about the impact of IFI involvement with poor countries would be for multilateral creditors to strengthen the "safety net" dimension of their programs by converting some of the debt owed them by poor-country governments into local-currency debt (rather than forgiving it outright). The repayments from this local-currency debt could be granted back to the debtor country to help boost spending on development projects, human capital investments (health, education, etc.), or poverty alleviation programs. Alternatively, they could be forgiven outright to encourage the borrower's attention to particular issues or if the inflow of local currency exceeds the amounts the IFIs can use. Moreover, ending the borrower's need to use often-scarce hard currency for multilateral debt payments would make those resources more available to the private sector. The multilaterals could make this expanded access a condition of their plan.

IN SUM

Debt relief will probably be more costly and the multilateral institutions will have to pay a higher share of the cost than the World Bank and the IMF now expect. Moreover, the process of forgiveness will need to be stretched over more time than either the IFIs or their critics assume if it is to be both affordable and effective.

In any case, reducing sub-Saharan Africa's debt-service burden is only a first step. The region needs new exports, new productive facilities, better communications/transportation infrastructure, and programs to expand worker productivity. Any debt-reduction plan that fails to take these needs into account is unlikely to be sustainable in the long run.

CHRISTINA KATSOURIS

"NEW DEBT DEAL FOR THE POOREST COUNTRIES"

Africa Recovery, December 1996

Finance Ministers Endorse IMF/World Bank Plan to Achieve "Sustainable" Levels of Debt

African finance ministers gave a qualified welcome to the debt initiative for Highly Indebted Poor Countries (HIPC) that was launched at the World Bank/International Monetary Fund (IMF) annual meetings in early October. They applauded the possibilities offered by a comprehensive scheme to reduce debt to manageable levels. But they also warned that uncertainties over funding, tough eligibility and performance criteria, and a long qualification period requiring sustained reform could result in help for too few countries, too late.

The plan is to tailor relief according to projections of each eligible country's export earnings, capital, and aid inflows. But as with earlier debt relief schemes, the HIPC initiative is available only to those countries with Bank and IMF-endorsed track records of good economic management and reform.

This makes it likely that few countries will be eligible for the full relief package, and some could wait six years for it. Others will have to make do with cuts and reschedulings of a portion of their bilateral debt and debt service by the Paris Club.

Creditors will evaluate each country's performance and debt relief needs over two distinct three-year periods. During the first three years (Phase 1), a government must establish a good track record of sound economic management under an IMF-enhanced structural adjustment facility (ESAF). The Paris Club will provide interim relief through annual rescheduling of debt-service, while the government keeps up with its debt payments to the Club.

In the third year of Phase 1, Bank and IMF staff and debtor government officials carry out preliminary analysis of the country's future export earnings and other inflows and measure this against future debt service obligations. They calculate whether a 67 percent cancellation of eligible Paris Club debt stock under the Naples terms would be enough to bring a country to "debt sustainability." This is defined as a debt-to-exports ratio of 200–250 percent, or an annual debt service-to-exports ratio under 20–25 percent, all at net present value.

If the projections show that a Naples debt stock reduction deal would help achieve sustainable levels of debt three years ahead, a country would be expected to settle for this deal, and receive no further relief.

In the case of a "borderline" country, for which it is doubted that existing mechanisms would bring debt sustainability in three years, the country can defer applying for a Naples deal and continue its ESAF into Phase 2. The Bank and Fund staff would ask their governing boards to endorse their conclusion that a country's debt would remain unsustainable and would circulate the analysis to other creditors. A Bank/Fund mission to the country, three months before the end of Phase 1, would seek agreement with the government on the findings.

Bank/Fund staff would then prepare an HIPC Board Document requesting help for the candidate. It would contain a final debt sustainability analysis, with proposals for sustainable debt-to-income ratios and for future support from other creditors. This document would then be endorsed at the end of the third year of Phase 1, known as the "decision point."

During Phase 2, qualifying countries would undergo another three years of surveillance and more sustainability studies, during which they would get exceptional grants and extra loans from the International Development Association (IDA), the Bank's concessional lending arm. These grants, an innovation for IDA, which, traditionally, provides only loans, aim to help a country sustain its reform programme and meet the criteria for debt reduction. It would not be used to buy back debt. Creditors would cancel some debt only at the end of Phase 2, known as the "completion point."

DIVERSITY OF SITUATIONS

The aim at completion point is to tailor relief packages to each debtor's needs. These could vary substantially, reflecting the diversity of debt profiles, range of creditors, obligations, and maturities.

If a country's bilateral debt appears unserviceable at completion point, the Paris Club would agree to cancel more of its eligible debt, from the current 67 percent up to a new maximum of 80 percent, and non–Paris Club bilateral creditors are expected to provide comparable treatment. If the multilateral debt burden poses unbearable strains, then portions of this debt would also be relieved.

In consultation with an HIPC government, creditors would set the target for the country's debt ratios after debt reduction to take account of critical factors such as the country's vulnerability to fluctuating export commodity prices.

Arguing for a shorter time-frame, critics say six years is intolerably long for a country to undergo strict surveillance and highly demanding reforms, while keeping up with debt payments. And these obligations would continue to accumulate before any debt reduction. If Mozambique, for example, had to wait the full six years, until 2003, its average annual debt service payments would more than triple, to $190.6 million from the $57 million paid in 1990–95, says the U.K.-based Debt Crisis Network.

Some advocates call for earlier relief and a delinkage from ESAFs, and urge the IMF to set less rigid performance criteria. The difficulties of meeting IMF targets for even three years are evident in the fact that only three African countries—Uganda, Burkina Faso, and Mali—have qualified for Naples debt stock reduction since the Paris Club, which uses similar criteria, began implementing Naples in February 1995.

However, the Bank and Fund make no apologies for the tough performance targets, arguing that most countries need to reform, and must show they can manage resources so effectively that they will not need to ask for further debt relief after benefiting from the HIPC deal.

They also point out that performance criteria include adequate investment in social sectors. Most important, the Bank and Fund say that the six-year time-frame is more of a guideline than a rigid rule and that interpretations will be flexible. For example, countries with current ESAF programmes will be considered as already in Phase 1, while countries with interrupted adjustment programmes will get some time credit for earlier progress. They emphasize the additional aid available in Phase 2, and that in exceptional cases, Phase 2 could be shortened for countries with a sustained track record.

FIRST QUALIFIERS

Reports indicate that debt sustainability analyses have begun for Uganda, Mali, and Burkina Faso, with creditors expected to reach the decision point on Uganda by March 1997. The initial focus seems to be on reviewing the debt relief needs of these countries to see if their exceptional situation—being the only African beneficiaries of Naples debt stock reduction—will bring them to sustainability.

Sustainability analyses are also under way for Ivory Coast and Mozambique, whose sound track records may qualify them for an early decision point. At the other extreme, troubled countries such as Zaire are likely to wait well beyond the six years.

Critics stress that the criteria for debt service and inflow projections alone would limit relief to too few countries. Analysts estimate that 19 sub-Saharan countries have debt-to-export ratios above 300 percent and that nine have ratios of 200 to 300 percent.

Yet the IMF suggested in September that only seven had unsustainable debt burdens and that a further nine were "possibly stressed" (see table below). Creditors stress that the September list was just preliminary, and that some countries could change categories with further analysis of likely resource inflows.

Political issues could also alter a country's prospects. Zambia is thought likely to be an early candidate for the HIPC deal. But some donors,

Table 1. Debt Ratios of Some Potentially Eligible African Countries (1995)

Unsustainable	Debt to Exports (%)	Debt Service to Exports[a] (%)
Burundi	689.2	25.2
Guinea-Bissau	1473.4	12.3
Mozambique	1388.7	23.0
Sao Tomé & Pr.	2032.9	22.1
Sudan	2908.0	0.1
Zaire	n.a.	n.a.
Zambia	556.6	31.3

Possibly Stressed	Debt to Exports (%)	Debt Service to Exports[a] (%)
Cameroon	321.7	16.5
Congo	489.2	51.5
Ivory Coast	580.9	40.1
Ethiopia	642.4	11.7
Madagascar	520.7	7.6
Niger	617.4	26.1
Rwanda	1871.2	12.5
Tanzania	870.7	20.4
Uganda	1008.5	44.0

[a] Actual payments
SOURCE: World Bank, World Debt Tables, *1996*.

dissatisfied with the government's conduct of recent elections, might withhold contributions to the Trust Fund to clear Zambia's obligations to the African Development Bank, aid sources say.

ENOUGH RELIEF FOR ENOUGH COUNTRIES?

Critics say another flaw of the plan is that it simply fails to provide enough relief for heavily indebted countries. Estimating total HIPC debt at $183 billion, Christian Aid, the U.K.-based NGO, calculates that some $87.1 billion of that is "unsustainable." It argues that a $5.7 billion cut (the lower range of the HIPC plan's cost) would account for only 6.4 percent of unsustainable debt, and 3 percent of total debt.

Looking at the potential impact of bilateral debt reduction, the European Network on Debt and Development (Eurodad) foresees patchy and far from impressive results from additional Paris Club relief. The Naples terms actually give far less relief than the well-publicized ceilings of 67 and 80 percent suggest, because loans contracted after a country's first rescheduling—known as the cut-off point—are not eligible for relief.

For example, Uganda's 1995 Naples deal canceled 67 percent of its eligible debt. But this accounted for only 17.4 percent of its total Paris Club debt, in part because most of this debt was contracted after Uganda's first rescheduling in 1981.

Eurodad estimates that the maximum relief likely for any country would be 54.4 percent of Paris Club debt—for Congo. At the other extreme, Burundi would get a 1.4 percent reduction on Club debt with a 67 percent deal, and a 1.6 percent reduction if the Club wrote off the maximum 80 percent. Such calculations have led to repeated calls for the Paris Club to cancel up to 90 percent of eligible debt stock, the figure originally proposed by the Bank and Fund to make the plan financially feasible. The Club has also been urged to move the cut-off point to a later date, to help countries sharing Uganda's predicament.

TEST FOR OTHER CREDITORS

Another area of uncertainty in the HIPC plan lies with non-Paris Club bilateral creditors and commercial banks. They have agreed in principle to the deal, but their preparedness to provide "at least comparable" debt relief will be tested in practice. The most notable creditors are the Russian Federation and Arab governments and multilateral institutions that together hold 83 percent of sub-Saharan Africa's non-OECD debt, says UNCTAD. They also account for over 75 percent of the subregion's debt-service obligations to the year 2000. The Russian Federation holds over half the bilateral debt of Angola, Ethiopia, and Mozambique and negotiations are stalled over the value in rubles of this debt. Russia argues for the old rate of $1=R 0.58, but the ruble had fallen to $1=R 5,069 by June 1996.

The Paris Club could put some pressure on bilaterals by making relief on their Paris Club debt conditional on their giving similar treatment to HIPCs. But since the Club has already canceled debt stock for some important creditors, its leverage could be limited.

With the ceiling set for now at 80 percent for all bilateral creditors, multilaterals will have to pick up a hefty tab in some cases. For Guinea-Bissau, with a total external debt of $816 million, a maximum 80 percent Paris Club stock reduction and comparable treatment from other bilaterals would shave only $126.8 million off the total. The country's exports earned $55.4 million in 1994, an exceptionally good year. Even if this improvement was sustained, multilaterals would still need to mobilize substantial amounts to lower the debt to a target range of $125–200 million.

The compliance of commercial creditors is also uncertain. Most are expected to cooperate easily on relief for the poorest countries, which owe them little. But they will probably show less enthusiasm for giving similar terms to those such as Ivory Coast, which has a hefty $2.7 billion commercial debt. The acid test should come later in 1997 when the Board Document solicits their opinions and contributions.

"HOW THE DEBT INITIATIVE WORKS"

Africa Recovery, December 1996

The IMF and World Bank initially costed the HIPC debt initiative at $5.7–$7.7 billion over the next decade, to be shared among bilateral, commercial, and multilateral creditors.

The Paris Club of official bilateral creditors was asked to provide some $2.9 billion by raising its maximum debt stock cancellation from 67 to 90 percent. The Club decided on 80 percent.

Other bilateral creditors are to provide comparable levels of relief on their assets at completion point through cancellation of debt stock.

Commercial creditors have yet to define how they will operate.

The World Bank's main participation will be through a Trust Fund administered by the International Development Association (IDA). As with other multilaterals, the Bank's charter prevents it from canceling debt, as this might damage their credit standing and raise their money market costs, which would be passed on to clients. To circumvent this, the Trust Fund is "off balance sheet," so funds can be channeled through it to HIPCs. The Trust can buy and then cancel a portion of multilateral debt; it can also pay principal and interest in advance or as it falls due. The Bank will put some of its net income into the Trust Fund, starting with $500 million (still to be paid in at the time of writing). Its Executive Board will have been asked to approve an additional $1.5 billion in coming years, "on a proportional basis with other contributors" and according to the Bank's share of a country's debt, Bank President James Wolfensohn said in October. Other multilateral and bilateral creditors will contribute to the Trust Fund. Their payments will also be used to buy back or repay debt owed to the African Development Bank, which cannot contribute because of its own financial difficulties.

The International Monetary Fund will participate mainly through its enhanced structural adjustment facility (ESAF) with a contribution of SDR 800 million. In a radical departure, the IMF will draw on ESAF money paid into escrow accounts to provide grants and loans with longer repayment periods (up to 20 years instead of the current ten-year maximum). Practical details have yet to be clarified, but in principle, the IMF will provide money on terms that translate into real grants.

It is also a "done deal," says Managing Director Michel Camdessus, that the IMF can in future sell up to 5 million ounces of gold to finance more debt relief, but "only when this need appears." Germany still objects, but the strong consensus of the Interim Committee in October, according to Mr. Camdessus, was that the Group of Seven invitation to the IMF to "optimize the management of its reserves" would entail selling some gold if and when needed.

NII K. BENTSI-ENCHILL

"DEBT RELIEF PROSPECTS WORRY AFRICAN MINISTERS"

Africa Recovery, January–April 1997

World Bank/IMF Seek to Reassure at ECA Conference

Voicing deep concerns, African finance ministers have called for more flexible application of the new Heavily Indebted Poor Countries (HIPC) debt-relief deal. They say "as many reforming African countries as possible" should have access to the HIPC package and urge the World Bank and International Monetary Fund (IMF) to make the six years of tough eligibility conditions shorter and less restrictive. The HIPC deal aims to reduce debts of eligible countries to "sustainable" levels.

At a March 31–April 2 conference in Addis Ababa, held by the U.N. Economic Commission for Africa (ECA), the ministers called for more rapid debt reduction for countries with a "demonstrated record of strong performance over a long period."

This was a reference to Uganda, which, on April 23, became the first country to get an HIPC deal. Uganda welcomed the debt relief, which will come in April 1998. It had earlier expressed disappointment at not getting debt relief this year, despite assurances of a 1997 date by the Bank and Fund. Oxfam, a U.K.-based nongovernmental organization, has charged that the Bank and Fund lack the political will to implement their own plan. Oxfam calculates that a one-year delay will cost Uganda $193 million, or six times its public-health spending. British parliamentarians of all parties in the Treasury Select Committee have in turn criticized the IMF for prevaricating on debt relief. The committee said on March 12 that the HIPC initiative was in danger of losing impetus and "must not be allowed to founder."

Against this background, debt and adjustment issues took center-stage in Addis Ababa, although financial sector reform, capacity building, and capital market development were the other conference themes. Uganda took every opportunity to make its case, while the Bank deployed Vice Presidents for Africa Callisto Madavo and Jean-Louis Sarbib, and the IMF fielded Mr. A. Basu, its Africa Region Deputy Director. They brought messages of optimism and faith in Africa's progress and stressed the need for sustained policy reforms.

But the conference tone was already set when Ethiopian Deputy Prime Minister Kassu Illala, in his opening speech, expressed doubts about the HIPC initiative's conditionality and eligibility criteria. On behalf of Prime Minister Meles Zenawi, Mr. Illala said that in almost all African countries, excessive debt is hampering efforts to attract resources required for basic development needs.

Without flexible application, the initiative could end up "like the mountain that gave birth to a mouse," said ECA Executive Secretary K.Y. Amoako. It "could look good on paper" but not benefit deserving African countries "genuinely burdened by debt," he added, noting the plan's "failure to consider the fiscal burden of debt as a central variable in the debt sustainability analysis." He also questioned the two three-year periods of successful adjustment that enable eligible HIPCs to qualify for final debt reduction, and whether adequate and timely financing has been committed, especially by bilateral donors.

Illustrating the ECA push for new methods of work, the conference format broke with the tradition of long speeches and little discussion. Instead, there were lively sessions featuring presentations by small panels, sharp questions and comments from ministers, central bankers, and senior officials, and detailed responses from panelists. This format, said Mr. Amoako, "exemplifies the new ECA, networking, showcasing African talent, facilitating substance, and helping Africa find new synergies."

KEY SESSION ON DEBT RELIEF

Uganda had wanted to bring a message of hope for a breakthrough to its fellow African countries "shackled by debt problems amidst widespread poverty," said Deputy Finance Minister Basoga Nsadhu, moderating the session on the HIPC initiative. But while the HIPC package is very welcome, some questions remain. These include the appropriateness of the eligibility criteria and whether the sustainability analyses give proper weight to vulnerability and other exogenous factors.

But for Mr. Jean-Louis Sarbib, the main issue was how to move forward, balancing divergent forces, to achieve a sustainable level of debt for the largest possible number of HIPCs. In a lucid presentation of the complex deal, he said the key achievement was that all creditors had agreed on a package for the totality of debt that provides an "exit strategy" from costly reschedulings and that also deals with the "moral hazard" of giving relief to potential backsliders by monitoring their performance over a number of years. The package would also preserve the Triple A rating of the multilateral financial institutions, said Mr. Sarbib, adding that in an era of dwindling resources, the HIPC deal would secure concessional funds that do not create new debt.

Only countries with per capita gross national product of $800 or less (known as "IDA-only" as they can borrow only from the World Bank's soft-loan arm, the International Development Association) with a track record of good adjustment are eligible for the deal. Only after "full use of existing mechanisms" could their debt be deemed unsustainable, and only then would HIPC relief kick in. There is no "predetermined list" of potential beneficiaries—the list published by the IMF last September "had caused problems"—and no country is in or out until its debt sustainability analysis has been endorsed by both Boards, Mr. Sarbib explained.

This vital debt sustainability analysis (DSA) is a tripartite exercise done by the Bank, the Fund, and the country near the end of the first three-year period. Appropriate speed has to be balanced with "ownership": a country "must be fully behind the DSA," Mr. Sarbib insisted.

[121]

The DSA is the basis for the "decision point" at the end of the third year, when creditors decide how much debt relief will be needed at the end of the sixth year, known as the "completion point." This second three-year period aims to ensure that the "budget space" provided by debt relief is applied to economic management and social development. A country starting a Bank/Fund programme in January 1997 would reach decision point in 1999 and completion point in 2002. If it already has a track record—hypothetically as far back as 1991—then the decision point could be in 1997 and an earlier completion point is "even possible," Mr. Sarbib said.

IDA grants may be given between decision and completion points, like a "down payment" that would "help keep all our eyes on the prize." Each creditor is responsible for its share of debt relief, and the bilaterals have so far put $43 million into the HIPC Trust Fund, Mr. Sarbib reported. The African Development Bank's initial contribution to the HIPC package is through the soft-loan African Development Fund (ADF), said ADB Vice President Ferhat Lounes. For the 1997–99 period, it is setting up a supplementary financing mechanism, similar to the World Bank's Fifth Dimension facility, to help deserving countries service debts contracted on harder terms from the ADB. Estimating HIPC debt to the ADB at $872 million in net present value and $1.3 billion in nominal terms, Mr. Lounes said ADB relief will be disbursed in the 1997–2003 period. The resources will come from ADB net revenue and from writing off bad ADF loans. But the ADB/ADF Boards are considering various options to fill a financing gap.

IMF participation is through its enhanced structural adjustment facility (ESAF), but special IMF funding will come only at completion point, said Mr. Basu. Just this past February did the IMF Board lift the previous country limit of two consecutive ESAFs— usually three years each—and set up an innovative Trust for Special ESAF Operations, which will make grants or interest-free, 10-to-20-year loans with a grace period of between five-and-a-half and ten years. He said most ESAF operations for HIPCs would involve grants paid into escrow accounts to cover debt-service payments. The IMF Board also decided on early transfers from the ESAF Reserve

Account to a Special Disbursement Account to get funds quickly to the first HIPC beneficiaries. But not all creditors have agreed to this.

HOW, WHEN, AND HOW MUCH?

Is there really enough money for a potentially growing number of HIPC beneficiaries, and besides the World Bank's initial promise of $500 million for the HIPC Trust Fund, how much are the IMF and bilateral creditors providing, asked Sudan's Central Bank Governor, Abdulla Hasan Ahmed.

Tanzania's Planning (and acting Finance) Minister, Daniel Yona said that six years of meeting tough performance criteria are just too long. The Bank and Fund's "traditional overcautiousness" explains why many of their programmes are not successful and why the HIPC initiative could fail, Mr. Yona said. Some governments have "behaved well for one or two years." but the critical external "helping hand" is just not there. The Paris Club has canceled "at most, one-eighth of our total debt" but Tanzania spends 40 percent of its budget on debt service, 40 percent on wages and salaries, leaving little for social services, Mr. Yona said, urging prompt help to maintain the pace of reform.

Why is there no reference to the level of internal debt in the basic HIPC hypotheses, asked Mr. Emmanuel Nana, Chief of Cabinet in the Central Bank of West African States (BCEAO), pointing to the influence of internal debt on savings and on investment. To spur growth, he noted, investment is meant to rise to some 25–30 percent of gross domestic product. He feared that the tough criteria may prevent the poorest HIPCs from getting even the little sums of relief they need. This stands in stark contrast to the immediate response and huge sums mobilized in 1996 to bail out Mexico, even without a proper economic programme.

Speakers from Sierra Leone and Guinea both pointed to the problem of using the total value of exports in the analysis of debt sustainability. They said that the major exports of some countries go through joint ventures with foreign firms. These firms make foreign payments and also transfer profits. Only export revenue actually accruing to the government should be considered, rather than the total value of exports, they argued.

Among other pertinent interventions, a Burkina Faso delegate reported some signs of withdrawal of bilateral support at the prospect of a country getting an HIPC deal. Uganda asked what categories of debt qualify and if there are cutoff dates. Another speaker asked if any of the first nine eligible HIPCs would benefit before the year 2000, adding that "as politicians, we have to advise our governments." Wishing that the question of adequate money for all eligible HIPCs was the only problem, Mr. Sarbib said it would not be easy to raise more resources. On the analysis of export revenue in the DSA, he gave strong assurances that such questions as the public share of export revenue will be answered during the case-by-case examination of the composition of exports. In Burkina Faso's case, the inclusion of workers' remittances as export revenue had put the country's debt burden in the "sustainable" category. Weak data on the remittances led to their subsequent exclusion and radically changed Burkina's debt profile. "You must make your case forcefully and we will listen. . . . But we must also listen to our Board members," Mr. Sarbib said.

Six years is an infinity for politicians, Mr. Sarbib agreed, but the HIPC package is "a real breakthrough," he said, recalling that "some of us were not allowed to utter the words 'multilateral debt relief' not so long ago."

The HIPC initiative covers public and publicly guaranteed debt, he explained, noting, for Sudan's benefit, that only private debt is discounted; there is no secondary market for publicly guaranteed debt and it retains its face value. To Guinea's concern over its debt to Russia, Mr. Sarbib mentioned the talks under way on Russia's contribution to debt relief at completion point. The impact of debt payments on the budget, a widespread African concern, is also being discussed, particularly in assessing country vulnerability.

Mr. Sarbib assured Uganda that Bank/Fund staff had made a strong case on its behalf; the Boards had listened and advanced the decision point, but the word on the completion point had not yet come down. Mr. Amoako observed that a one- or two-year delay in reaching completion point could mean less relief for Uganda. Mr. Sarbib agreed this was true in that a more distant completion point means less debt to repay and less relief needed.

The exact usage of the Bank's HIPC Trust Fund is yet to be decided, Mr. Sarbib said, but the intention is to use IDA grants as quickly as possible. He stressed that any hesitancy on his part is due to an "excess, not a lack, of transparency." He just did not have all the answers and "we are learning by doing." Mr. Basoga Nsadhu of Uganda heartily supported this Bank acknowledgment of room for improvement and that "we are all students."

ISSUES OF MULTILATERAL FINANCE

The working sessions began with presentations by the World Bank, ADB, and IMF on the role of multilateral financial institutions in Africa's growth and development. Panelists for other sessions included Dr. Chris Stals, South African Reserve Bank governor, Mr. Nana of BCEAO, and Dr. Benno Ndulu, African Economic Research Consortium Executive Director, on financial sector reform; Mr. John Ross, Vice President of New York Bay Associates, and Dr. A. Maruping, Governor of Lesotho's Central Bank, on building and using African capacity for debt management; and Dr. Lemma Senbet, University of Maryland, Mr. Arnold Ekpe, Chief Executive Officer of ECOBANK, and Mr. George Akamiokhor, Director-General of Nigeria's Securities and Exchange Commission, on capital market development and the role of information technology.

Africa is looking better, said Mr. Madavo, its output up from 0.9 percent in 1994 to 5.6 percent in 1996 and 31 countries now with positive per capita growth. These gains are fragile and reforms have to be deepened and accelerated, but there is no reason why Africa should not set ambitious growth targets of 8 or 9 percent.

The Bank's first principle in Africa is to support the new-style political leadership and foster ownership of economic reform. The Bank, Mr. Madavo said, "can't enforce or buy reform in Africa" but must support Africa's own efforts to achieve progress in all areas, including regional integration and human resource development. "The Bank can't go it alone," he declared, stressing the importance of partnership and citing the Bank's major role in the U.N. System-wide Special Initiative on Africa.

Despite some problems, the Bank's International Development Association (IDA) maintains its critical role by disbursing each year some $2.5 billion of concessional loans to Africa, not to mention the $5 billion raised through the Special Programme of Assistance for Africa (SPA-4) for the next four years. But undisbursed IDA funds now stand at some $8.5 billion due to implementation problems in some of the 500-odd projects under way in Africa.

Among the comments from the audience, Zambia's Finance Minister, Roland Penza, urged the Bank to take a much keener interest in such problematic areas as public-sector reform and retrenchments. Mr. Madavo agreed there are few examples of successful public-sector reform, and agreed on the need to "look again" at policy in this area.

There is always routine support for regional integration, noted Mr. Boubacar Ba, Deputy Executive Secretary (Economic Affairs) of the Economic Community of West African States (ECOWAS). But regional structures are inadequately financed and multilateral development banks are so oriented toward individual states that the latter need the banks' assent to contribute to some regional programmes. Will the multilateral banks get closer in concrete ways to regional structures in the short term?

The World Bank has not felt it possesses the right instruments, Mr. Madavo said. Using the example of the Maputo Corridor, he wondered if the Bank should make a loan to South Africa and a credit to Mozambique. The Bank is open to ideas, particularly from staff of the regional organizations, "so let's worry together" about how to proceed, he said.

On resource mobilization, Mr. Basu said unnecessary tax hikes prompt more tax evasion. It is better, he said, to improve collection, limit exemptions, and shift resources from low-priority areas "to those on which the multilaterals have been insisting, such as health and education."

CHRISTINA KATSOURIS

"DEBT RELIEF DELAY FOR POOREST COUNTRIES"

Africa Recovery, January–April 1997

Uganda to Get Relief Next Year, Major Creditors
Insist on Tougher Conditions

Uganda will get a reduction of $338 million in the present value of its external debt in April 1998. It is the first beneficiary of the Heavily Indebted Poor Countries (HIPC) Initiative, the World Bank and International Monetary Fund (IMF) said in Washington on April 23. The plan aims to reduce foreign debts of eligible countries to "sustainable" levels. Present value of Uganda's total external debt is nearly $1.9 billion.

Describing the deal as "warmly welcome," Uganda's Minister of Planning and Economic Development, Richard Kaijuka, said the international community had recognized the country's achievements of the last decade and also the "need to ensure that debt payments do not constrain further progress," a World Bank press release reported.

Prior to this decision, Uganda had seemed on track for debt relief this year. It then became known in March that major creditors were suggesting April 1998 at the earliest, others November 1998, and others still 1999. The Ugandan government made clear its disappointment and reiterated its need for prompt relief. In an early March letter to a London newspaper, Uganda's Finance Minister, J.S. Mayanja Nkangi, said third- or fourth-quarter 1997 dates were explicitly discussed at last October's World Bank/IMF meetings. Uganda was "increasingly frustrated" at the prospect of delay, he wrote.

Launched in October 1996, the HIPC plan aims to provide relief for eligible countries with strong IMF/Bank programmes and with foreign debt burdens deemed "unsustainable" even after getting debt-stock reduction from bilateral creditors, mainly in the Paris Club.

The first package to enlist all categories of creditors, it aims to reduce and restructure bilateral, commercial, and previously untouchable multilateral debt to levels that enable HIPCs to pay debt service and also invest in socioeconomic development. This "exit strategy" is to free countries from repeated and costly rescheduling. Once a country exits, it cannot ask for more debt relief.

A country must normally complete six years of successful IMF/World Bank adjustment to qualify. Toward the end of the first three-year period, Bank and IMF staff do a "debt sustainability analysis" (DSA), using 20-year projections of debt, debt service, and income. This forms the basis, at the end of the third year, for the "decision point" when creditors agree on how much relief to grant at the end of the sixth year "completion point."

Under various pressures, the Fund and Bank have modified this six-year schedule, enabling rare countries such as Uganda to qualify for an early decision point and a shorter gap between decision and completion.

While creditors have now agreed to an April 1997 decision point for Uganda, Bank officials earlier conceded there was a "tension" over the date for granting it actual debt relief. U.S. Treasury officials privately argued that additional aid and later completion would enhance the success of Uganda's reforms. "Is it a more constructive way . . . to provide money more quickly, to get the deal done . . . or is it more effective to wait a little longer," reinforce the current programme and then reduce the debt, asked Mr. Jim Adams, a Bank country director for Uganda and Tanzania. Bank officials have avoided naming specific creditors, but some argue that early completion for Uganda could set a precedent that would raise unrealistic expectations for other HIPC candidates.

KEY DOCUMENT ON UGANDA

The preliminary HIPC document recommending Uganda's eligibility was presented by Bank and IMF staff to their Boards for initial discussion on 10–12 March. It argues that Uganda is eligible for relief under most HIPC criteria: its $270 per capita gross national product in 1996 qualifies it on poverty grounds, as does its adjustment track record on policy grounds.

By mid-1996, Uganda's net present value (NPV) of debt—the sum of all future debt service obligations on current debt discounted at market interest rates to reflect concessionality—was $1.64 billion, or nearly 233 percent of exports.

The document uses a baseline scenario with debt and debt service ratios based on projected growth of gross domestic product (GDP), exports, other income flows, and outlays. Then a sensitivity analysis works out how changes in income or outlays may alter Uganda's debt ratios and payment capacity. The baseline scenario assumes that real GDP will grow by 7 percent between June 1996 and June 1999, and by 5 percent a year thereafter. The analysis projects that the NPV debt/exports ratio would rise to 254 percent in fiscal 1996/97, fall to 208 percent in 2005/06, and 153 percent by 2015. The debt service ratio would steadily fall below 20 percent in 1999/2000 to 13.5 percent by 2005/06 and then stabilize near 11 percent.

The document says that Uganda, which got 66.4 percent of its export earnings in 1995 from coffee, is more vulnerable than all other HIPC countries bar Congo, in terms of export concentration and volatility of export revenue. For example, a 20 percent fall in coffee prices below baseline projections could raise the NPV of debt to exports by 30–40 percentage points over the 1996/97 baseline to 282 percent and keep it above 250 percent until 2005/06. It would remain above 200 percent until 2015/16.

Given this vulnerability, Uganda might have difficulty servicing its debts at the higher end of the HIPC guidelines' target range of 200–250 percent for the NPV debt/exports ratio. The paper recommended 200–220 percent as an appropriate "sustainability target" to reduce the risk of further debt problems.

A 200 percent target implies debt relief of $385 million at an April 1998 completion point—$311 million from multilateral creditors and $74.7 million from bilaterals. A target of 220 percent would require $189.5 million in multilateral relief and $62 million from bilaterals.

Additional Tables

Table 1. External Debt Table

	Total External Debt ($million)			Long-Term Debt/ Total Debt (%)	Distribution of Total External Debt (%)			External Debt as % of		Debt Service as % of Exports of Goods & Services
					Multilateral	Bilateral	Private	GNP	Exports of Goods & Services	
	1980	1990	1995	1995	1995	1995	1995	1995	1995	1995
Algeria	19,365	27,896	32,610	93	11.6	35.3	45.57	83.1	264.2	38.7
Angola		8,443	11,482	83	1.7	18.3	63.08	274.9	314.3	12.5
Benin	424	1,245	1,646	92	52.3	39.6	0	81.8	285.6	8.4
Botswana	147	563	699	98	68	23.5	6.86	16.3	24	3.2
Burkina Faso	330	834	1,267	90	77.6	11.7	0	55	346.1	11.1
Burundi	166	907	1,457	95	80.1	14.3	0	110.1	829.3	27.7
Côte d'Ivoire	7,462	17,259	18,952	77	20.6	28.5	28.49	251.7	418.6	23.1
Cameroon	2,588	6,679	9,350	88	17.9	58.1	12.32	124.4	338.3	20.1
Cape Verde Islands		135	216	86	68.8	16.3	0.86	56		
Central African Rep.	195	699	944	90	67.2	21.6	1.80		403.9	6.8
Chad	285	530	908	92	73	19.3	0	81.4	339	5.9
Comoros		185	203	92	75.4	17.5	0			
Congo	1,526	4,953	6,052	82	11.7	54.9	15.58	365.8	481.8	14.4
Congo (Zaire)		10,270	13,137	73	18.3	48.2	5.57	255		
Djibouti		206	260	84	52.9	31.1	0			
Egypt, Arab Rep.	19,131	33,402	34,116	93	12.4	74.4	5.58	73.3	208.1	14.6
Equatorial Guinea		241	293	78	34.3	38.2	5.46	196		
Ethiopia (incl. Eritrea)	824	3,809	5,221	95	45.3	41.8	7.60	99.9	458.2	13.6
Gabon	1,514	3,984	4,492	91	14.6	71.9	4.55	121.6	160.3	15.8
Gambia, The	137	369	426	90	76	14.4	0		235.1	14

Table 1. External Debt Table (continued)

	Total External Debt ($million)			Long-Term Debt/Total Debt (%)	Distribution of Total External Debt (%)			External Debt as % of		Debt Service as % of Exports of Goods & Services
					Multilateral	Bilateral	Private	GNP	Exports of Goods & Services	
	1980	1990	1995	1995	1995	1995	1995	1995	1995	1995
Ghana	1,398	3,873	5,874	78	50.8	19.5	7.80	95.1	366.5	23.1
Guinea	1,134	2,476	3,242	92	45.2	44.2	2.76	91.2	453.4	25.3
Guinea-Bissau	145	712	894	95	56.1	39	0	353.7	1,874.3	66.9
Kenya	3,383	7,056	7,381	86	39.5	31	15.48	97.7	248.2	25.7
Lesotho	72	395	659	93	69.6	18.6	4.65	44.6	108.8	6
Liberia	1,241	1,849	2,127	55	21.5	23.7	9.90	141.7	562.2	9.2
Madagascar		3,720	4,302	86	39.2	44.7	1.72	166.8	499.6	25.9
Malawi	821	1,579	2,140	92	78.8	12.9	0.92	131.9	467.1	12.6
Mali	732	2,502	3,066	93	45.2	47.4	0			
Mauritania	843	2,141	2,467	89	36.8	51.6	0	243.3	458.5	21.5
Mauritius	467	995	1,801	81	15	23.5	42.93	45.9	75	9
Morocco	9,247	23,527	22,147	98	30.8	41.2	26.46	71	200.9	32.1
Mozambique		4,665	5,781	92	22.7	67.2	1.84	443.6	1,192.5	35.3
Namibia										
Niger	863	1,793	1,633	92	53.2	31.3	8.28	91.2	571.7	19.8
Nigeria	8,921	33,440	35,005	83	14.1	44.8	24.07	140.5	274.5	12.3
Rwanda	190	711	1,008	94	80.4	14.1	0	89.1	657.3	
Sao Tome Principe		153	277	94	65.8	28.2	0	693		
Senegal	1,473	3,731	3,845	84	48.4	32.8	3.36	82.3	224.3	18.7
Seychelles		195	164	92	38.6	40.5	13.80	34		

Table 1. External Debt Table (continued)

	Total External Debt ($million)			Long-Term Debt/ Total Debt (%)	Distribution of Total External Debt (%)			External Debt as % of		Debt Service as % of Exports of Goods & Services
					Multilateral	Bilateral	Private	GNP	Exports of Goods & Services	
	1980	1990	1995	1995	1995	1995	1995	1995	1995	1995
Sierra Leone	435	1,206	1,225	79	34.3	44.2	0	159.7	1,163.5	60.3
Somalia		2,370	2,673	73	29.2	42.3	1.46	284		
South Africa										
Sudan		*14,762*	17,623	58	12.2	32.5	-3.34	*169*		
Swaziland		262	251	94	48.9	45.1	0	24		
Tanzania	2,460	6,286	7,333	84	39.1	39.5	5.88	207.4	585.2	17.4
Togo	1,052	1,286	1,486	87	48.4	34.8	3.48	121.2	464.5	5.7
Tunisia	3,527	7,691	9,933	91	37.2	35.5	18.20	57.3	113.2	17
Uganda	689	2,583	3,564	86	61.8	21.5	2.58	63.7	555.1	21.3
Zambia	3,261	7,265	6,853	74	31.9	40	2.22	191.3	528.7	174.4
Zimbabwe	786	3,247	4,885	77	33.1	23.9	23.02	78.9		25.6

NOTE: Figures in italics are for years other than those specified.

SOURCES: "Table 17: External Debt," *Selected World Development Indicators 1997.* (Internet address: http://ftp.worldbank.org/html/iecdd/wdipdf.htm).
"Table: External Debt," *Global Development Finance, 1997.* The World Bank. pp. 10–12.

Table 2. African Debt to U.S. Government: Outstanding Long-Term Principal Indebtedness of Foreign Countries on U.S. Government Credits[a] as of December 31, 1994[b]

(in millions of dollars and dollar equivalents)

	Under Export-Import Bank Act	Under Foreign Assistance (and related acts)	Under Agricultural Trade, Development & Assistance Act — Loans of Foreign Currency to: Foreign Gov'ts	Private Enterprise	Long-Term Dollar Credits	Lend Lease Surplus Property & Other War Accounts[c]	Commodity Credit Corp. Export Credit	TOTAL
Algeria	207.3							207.3
Angola	13.6				7.9			21.5
Botswana		21.4						21.4
Cameroon	43.9	7.3						51.2
Central African Republic	6							6
Congo	11.8				16.7			28.5
Côte d'Ivoire	152.2	25.5	0.5		65			243.2
Ethiopia		80.7	0.1		1.1			81.9
Gabon	54.5	7.1						61.6
Ghana			*					*
Guinea	8.8		9.8		97.6			116.2
Kenya	74.3	43.9						118.2
Liberia	6	93.9			91.9	12.7		204.4
Madagascar	24.4							24.4
Mali			*					*

Country								Total
Mauritania	6.6							6.6
Mauritius	2.8				5.6			8.4
Morocco	93	318.3	9.4	2	508.2	135.8		1,066.7
Mozambique	47.2							47.2
Niger	6.8	4						10.8
Nigeria	709.2							709.3
Senegal	1.6	12.4	0.7					14.6
Sierra Leone	13.5				61.9			75.4
Somalia		85.6			146.8			232.4
Sudan	28.2	139.8			386.9	61.2		616.2
Swaziland		9.3						9.3
Tanzania	28							28
Togo	*							*
Tunisia	20.7	122.2	11.8	7.4	153.1			315.1
Uganda	1.3							1.3
Zaire	921.8	283.6			283.8	12.4		1,501.7
Zambia	143.1	3			129			275
Zimbabwe		4			51			55
Africa Total:	2,626.4	1,262.0	32.3	9.4	2,006.4	209.5	12.7	6,158.6

NOTES: *Designates less than $50,000. Detail may not add to totals due to rounding.

aExclusive of indebtedness arising from World War I.

bIncludes estimates for the U.S. dollar equivalent of receivables denominated in other than dollars and/or payable at the option of the debtor in foreign currencies, goods or services. The total amount of such estimates approximates $255.2 million as of December 31, 1994. Long-term loans and credits have an original maturity of more than 1 year.

cExcludes outstanding interest deferred by formal agreement or in arrears, but includes capitalized interest.

SOURCE: U.S. Department of the Treasury.

OTHER REPORTS OF INDEPENDENT TASK FORCES SPONSORED BY THE COUNCIL ON FOREIGN RELATIONS

* †*Differentiated Containment: U.S. Policy Toward Iran and Iraq* (1997)
Zbigniew Brzezinski and Brent Scowcroft, Co-Chairs

†*Russia, Its Neighbors, and an Enlarging NATO* (1997)
Richard G. Lugar, Chair

* †*Financing America's Leadership: Protecting American Interests and Promoting American Values* (1997)
Mickey Edwards and Stephen J. Solarz, Co-Chairs

**Rethinking International Drug Control: New Directions for U.S. Policy* (1997)
Mathea Falco, Chair

†*A New U.S. Policy Toward India and Pakistan* (1997)
Richard N. Haass, Chairman; Gideon Rose, Project Director

Arms Control and the U.S.-Russian Relationship: Problems, Prospects, and Prescriptions (1996)
Robert D. Blackwill, Chairman and Author; Keith W. Dayton, Project Director

American National Interests and the United Nations (1996)
George Soros, Chairman

Making Intelligence Smarter: The Future of U.S. Intelligence (1996)
Maurice R. Greenberg, Chairman; Richard N. Haass, Project Director

Lessons of the Mexican Peso Crisis (1996)
John C. Whitehead, Chairman; Marie-Josée Kravis, Project Director

Non-Lethal Technologies: Military Options and Implications (1995)
Malcolm H. Wiener, Chairman

Managing the Taiwan Issue: Key is Better U.S. Relations with China (1995)
Stephen Friedman, Chairman; Elizabeth Economy, Project Director

Should NATO Expand? (1995)
Harold Brown, Chairman; Charles Kupchan, Project Director

Success or Sellout?: The U.S.-North Korean Nuclear Accord (1995)
Kyung Won Kim and Nicholas Platt, Chairmen; Richard N. Haass, Project Director

Nuclear Proliferation: Confronting the New Challenges (1995)
Stephen J. Hadley, Chairman; Mitchell B. Reiss, Project Director

---

*Available from Brookings Institution Press ($5.00 per copy).To order, call 1-800-275-1447.

†Available on the Council on Foreign Relations homepage at www. foreignrelations.org.